Reaching and Teaching *All* Instrumental Music Students

Second Edition

Kevin Mixon

Published in partnership with
MENC: The National Association for Music Education

ROWMAN & LITTLEFIELD EDUCATION
A division of
ROWMAN & LITTLEFIELD PUBLISHERS, INC.
Lanham • New York • Toronto • Plymouth, UK

Published in partnership with MENC:
The National Association for Music Education

Published by Rowman & Littlefield Education
A division of Rowman & Littlefield Publishers, Inc.
A wholly owned subsidary of The Rowman & Littlefield Publishing Group, Inc.
4501 Forbes Boulevard, Suite 200, Lanham, Maryland 20706
http://www.rowmaneducation.com

Estover Road
Plymouth PL6 7PY
United Kingdom

British Library Cataloguing in Publication Information Available

Library of Congress Cataloging-in-Publication Data

Mixon, Kevin.
Reaching and teaching all instrumental music students / Kevin Mixon. 2nd edition
p. cm.
"Published in partnership with MENC: The National Association for Music
Education."
Includes bibliographical references.
ISBN 978-1-60709-906-2 (cloth : alk. paper) — ISBN 978-1-60709-907-9 (pbk. : alk.
paper) — ISBN 978-1-60709-908-6 (ebook)
 1. Music—Instruction and study. 2. Musical instruments—Instruction and
study. I. MENC: The National Association for Music Education (U.S.) II. Title.
MT1.M68 2011
784.071—dc22
 2011008651

♾™ The paper used in this publication meets the minimum requirements of
American National Standard for Information Sciences—Permanence of Paper for
Printed Library Materials, ANSI/NISO Z39.48-1992.

Printed in the United States of America

This book is dedicated with
love to my mother, Barbara Anne McCoy,
whose lifelong teaching and learning serve
as continual inspiration.

Contents

Foreword

Every person who ever made the decision to become a music teacher has done so with the goal of imparting upon their students the love and joy of making music. Sharing their love of music with eager, willing, and compliant children is the goal. These teachers have in their minds what they consider the great masterworks that all students should know and be exposed to. They have formed their philosophies of what they think is good music and how they will share these values with their students. What they don't understand is that they have developed these philosophies, opinions, and teaching skills based upon teaching in an ideal situation. Many would say ideal situations do not exist, but there are certainly good situations with adequate funding, rehearsal time, and support, plus a certain type of student demographic that has become the model for programs around the country.

The problem is what to do when the program you have does not meet these expectations. Unfortunately many teachers who find themselves in these types of situations quickly give up on their high standards of musical achievement and also give up on this different demographic of students. Many get to the point where they feel they are just trying to survive. Their goal of imparting the love and joy of music goes right out the window. They come to the conclusion that these students don't want to learn or can't learn, or they make all types of excuses as to why reaching a high level of music performance at these types of schools is just not possible. Couple all of these perceived roadblocks with the fact that teachers have been ill prepared to deal with these types of situations in their own education, and we have a recipe for disaster in the classroom.

In my own experience in the classroom over the years, I have struggled with these same issues. There have been students I have had difficulty reaching using the standard or traditional methods of teaching. There were students who did not like or want to learn the music that I thought was appropriate. There were students who gave me the impression that they didn't care or want to learn. All of these conclusions were based upon my own biases or lack of understanding of the ways to successfully teach these types of students. It was easiest to just give up on them, but if we don't find a way to inspire and teach these students, who will?

Reaching and Teaching All *Instrumental Music Students* shows us that it is possible to teach and reach these students. It is written from the perspective of someone who has been there and has been able to find a way to do it. Mr. Mixon's clear and informative prose gives the reader a wealth of real-world solutions. The book details strategies that have worked, along with suggestions and methods of teaching to all students in all types of instrumental programs, even those who most would categorize as difficult or less-than-ideal situations. It will also help the teacher who may happen to be in a good situation but wants help in teaching challenging students.

Committed and creative teachers who place a value on every student they touch, not just the easy-to-teach ones, will make the difference in the lives of their students. Don't let the opportunity to share your love of music with every student be impeded by a lack of understanding. Use *Reaching and Teaching* All *Instrumental Music Students* as a resource to help you, inspire you, and teach you that all students do matter and can be inspired through music. Most important, don't give up on your students or on your musical integrity, but do alter your approach to fit the needs of your students so that all of them can strive for musical excellence no matter where they live or what school they happen to attend. You will find the greater the challenge, the greater the reward. Instead of wishing for a prestigious teaching job in that better-funded school district, do your best with what you have for the sake of your students. You owe it to your students and yourself to do so.

—Larry Clark
Vice President and Editor-in-Chief
Carl Fischer Music

Acknowledgments

I would like to thank the following teachers for their helpful advice while writing this book: Bob and Pam Phillips, Alfred Publishing; Jill DiBattista, string teacher, West Genesee School District, Camillus, New York; Jeanne Porcino Dolamore, Poughkeepsie City School District, New York; and Rebecca Pena, general music teacher, Syracuse City School District. My thanks also to Steve Frank, instrumental music teacher, West Genesee School District and Onondaga Community College, Syracuse, New York, for allowing me to include his instructional game. I am also indebted to these outstanding colleagues for reviewing final drafts of the book: Robert Sheldon, Carol Frierson-Campbell, Sandra Dackow, Bob Phillips, Edward S. Lisk, and Larry Clark.

Thanks also to *The Instrumentalist*, the National Association of Music Merchants, and the Music Achievement Council for permission to reproduce materials and the Conn-Selmer Company for assistance in researching aptitude tests.

Finally, I am grateful for the patience of my two children, Chelsea and Kevin Jr., who often put their immediate needs aside and gave me time to complete this book. I am blessed and proud beyond words to have such great kids.

Introduction:
New Perspectives

NEW EXEMPLARS: MOVING AWAY FROM THE SUBURBS

Well-funded and supported instrumental music programs have had the spotlight for so long that many directors have come to believe that high-quality instruction and high student achievement can only take place in ideal circumstances. Much of the current educational literature applies theories and techniques to model instrumental ensembles, but directors cannot always emulate these circumstances.

Model ensembles often represent well-funded suburban school districts (though not all suburban schools are affluent, of course). Though excellent teaching and learning takes place in these programs, using them as instructional examples has obvious limits. Many schools do not have the same economic advantages, schedules, or types of student needs, particularly in urban or rural areas.

Rather than pit teaching in the field against the educational decrees of the ivory tower, this book aims to take small doses of the valuable research conducted in the hallowed halls of academia and integrate it with the less-than-ideal circumstances in real classrooms.

"Less than ideal" doesn't mean "urban." It means not enough instruments. It means cuts in rehearsal time. It means having to teach to a broad range of learning styles at once.

I have written this book to address issues that many instrumental music texts might overlook. Many academics hypothesize, postulate, and theorize without any experience in challenging classrooms. Such academic work is important, and throughout this book I cite scholars, researchers, and master teachers from whom I have "borrowed," and I hope you will consult these sources directly as well as consider how I have adapted these methods to suit my personal education philosophy and unique teaching environment. I have distilled their ideas, philosophies, and theories down to one thing: How could this work in my classroom? I hope you will do the same with this book.

I have adapted well-known approaches to work within the constraints surrounding my instrumental music programs. Because the following strategies are often borne of my own experience and tempered with personal philosophy and values, they do not have universal application without modifications.

NEW STRATEGIES: BUILDING A STRONG FOUNDATION

The first two chapters, "Getting Students Started" and "Maintaining Interest," discuss effective ways to recruit and retain students with strategies that have relevance in most educational environments.

General strategies may need to adapt to certain environments, such as in urban schools. For example, in Chapter 3, "Gaining Support," I show how, regardless of socioeconomic circumstances, parental support is vital to instrumental music programs, but I give additional ways directors might get support to serve diverse students and their families. Many people wrongly assume that parents in less affluent communities have less concern for their children's education. This assumption is categorically false, based on both my own experiences and academic research. Researchers repeatedly report the strength of familial bonds and the importance of garnering support from parents for academic achievement in urban schools (Hale, 2001; Kuykendall, 1992; Wilson & Corbett, 2001).

NEW WAYS OF TEACHING

In an educational era where cutbacks have become commonplace, directors must make the most of what they have. In Chapter 4, I address a key issue facing most music programs: lack of instructional time. Instead of lamenting increasing time constraints, I offer practical ways in which directors can maximize their rehearsal through effective time and student management.

Making every minute of rehearsal productive for all students means you must teach all students according to the ways in which they learn. Embracing diverse students, situations, and music requires an acceptance of diverse learning styles and needs, a topic I explore in Chapter 5, "Multisensory Teaching." I show specific ways in which teachers can teach fundamental musical concepts to all students.

NEW STUDENTS: EXCEPTIONAL LEARNERS

Regardless of economics or diversity, all directors need to make ensembles accessible—and rewarding—to exceptional learners. Aside from the fact that legislation mandates inclusion, a mission that promotes music for all children dictates that it is simply the right thing to do. In many programs, exceptional learners gain membership only when parents and other advocates seek access.

But you can welcome exceptional learners without compromising the quality of performing ensembles, which many directors fear. Because special education is usually not an area of expertise for directors, a collegial approach that involves special education staff and parental input is the key to success. In time, directors become comfortable with working with exceptional learners and realize their value as ensemble members.

NEW ACTIVITIES: IMPROVISATION AND COMPOSITION

The National Standards set forth by MENC: The National Association for Music Education consider improvisation and composition as vital components of a complete, comprehensive music education in general, choral, and instrumental music settings (MENC, 1994). Directors often sacrifice opportunities for improvisation and composition in order to focus on performance, an equally creative endeavor (Reimer, 1989, p. 71), though different in many respects. Lack of experience, texts, other (often costly) resources, and instruction time requires easily implemented improvisation and composition activities that actually support and enhance performance goals. I devote Chapter 8 entirely to improvisation and composition and present efficient activity ideas that tap students' creativity. My musical mission is that you will take what you can from this book and adapt it to your unique classroom to teach and reach all instrumental music students.

One

Getting Students Started

Though recruiting practices vary, successful program building depends upon carefully matching students to instruments by considering their aptitude and preferences. Many administrators and other policymakers measure instrumental program value by the size of enrollment in ensembles, and many directors believe that as many students as possible deserve the opportunity to play an instrument. Pragmatically, instrumental music programs depend on large recruitment numbers because the number of student participants tends to decrease in higher grade levels. Recruiting many students is crucial, but take care in how you introduce these students to instrumental music.

Many directors successfully recruit large numbers of students with very little enticement. Many younger students are already excited about learning to play an instrument without much of a sales pitch from the ensemble director. Holding recruiting sessions to generate interest is important nonetheless. These sessions are useful also for matching interested students with instruments that complement their abilities—thereby increasing the likelihood of students' success and decreasing the rate of attrition.

Successful recruiting depends upon knowing how to deal with people. A fine arts administrator recently said that the two most important qualities he looked for when hiring new music teachers were musical competence and people skills. Every aspect of instrumental music teaching, program building, and maintenance depends upon interacting with people in a way that fosters long-term musical study.

Many directors hold an evening meeting for parents and students that provides an opportunity for them to meet with instrument dealers and to fill out necessary forms. Prior to this parental meeting, consider planning smaller, more informal meetings for students during the school day, with only one or two classrooms at a time (no more than fifty students). These sessions allow prospective students to see instruments "up close," hear those instruments demonstrated by the director or current students, and ask more questions. Smaller sessions also generate fewer behavior management issues.

Directors might consider scheduling these recruiting sessions judiciously at the beginning or end of the school year, when classroom teachers can more conveniently send both prospective students and current students. Directors can "sweeten the deal" by supervising these sessions themselves so that classroom teachers get an extra, well-deserved break. (I have found this to be quite a motivator, particularly at the end of the school year!) Directors might schedule sessions during general music classes, particularly if they integrate them with a unit on instrument families. Though you can demonstrate instruments in many ways, recruitment sessions simply must include demonstrations to help students decide what instruments they prefer.

Individual students have unique skills and preferences, which obviously affect their choices. Unfortunately, some directors let students and their parents select instruments entirely on their own. Although student preference is paramount, selecting an instrument without advice from a knowledgeable director may lead to students quitting. Despite their best efforts, students mismatched with an instrument may trail behind their peers because the instrument is too hard to play. This lack of progress may lead to an unnecessary instrument switch later in the year or, even worse, a loss of interest in instrumental music altogether.

Instrument selection without director guidance also leads to unbalanced ensemble instrumentation and reduced sonority and repertoire selection, restricting enriching musical experiences for all students. Once initiated, this imbalance may stay with the same group for several years as students advance together.

You can avoid losing prospective players by considering four components important to the recruiting process: instrument demonstration, skills assessment, dissemination of the information letter, and tone production assessment.

INSTRUMENT DEMONSTRATION

Typical recruiting sessions include demonstrations by the director or by current students. Even if you use a commercial demonstration video, display real instruments and show students how they are played. Presuming your playing proficiency will give a favorable impression of the instrument, introducing prospective students to unfamiliar instruments, and reminding them about familiar ones are crucial factors in matching students to instruments.

Instrument timbres are particularly important to beginners. Edwin Gordon (1997) suggests, "Although elementary school students may be attracted initially to an instrument because of its appearance or other irrelevant reasons, ultimately they find the most success when they play an instrument that has a tone quality that appeals to them" (p. 274). Though experience has shown me that other factors need consideration as well when selecting instruments, demonstrating instruments for prospective students helps them decide which instrument timbres they prefer.

Using current instrumental music students to demonstrate instruments is even more effective than demonstrating them yourself. Prospective students are interested in how "real kids" perform. Current students enjoy introducing prospective students to an activity in which they themselves are proud to participate.

Reasonably proficient demonstrators close in age to your prospective students show students that early success on an instrument is certainly possible (such as fifth graders demonstrating for fourth graders). Ending the playing demonstration with a favorite piece from the most recent concert emphasizes the progress that can be made in a short time, often within a single school year.

Because student demonstrators are still new players, I use several students (rather than a soloist) on each instrument because it generates a more satisfactory sound from most beginner groups. Except for the final piece that I conduct, I play along with students on all of the different instruments in addition to my role as presenter. I find that using proficient second-year students for recruiting sessions works quite well. You may want to consider using advanced students as demonstrators, but students from middle or junior high and high schools may pose transportation, scheduling, and other logistical problems arising with multiple recruiting sessions.

SKILLS ASSESSMENT

A portion of the recruiting session should include assessing the skills of prospective students, and I use short tests such as those provided by instrument purveyors.

While most of these tests do not measure aptitude with the precision of more rigorously researched aptitude tests, they can assist directors with instrument selection, particularly with wind and percussion instruments. In some cases, good scores on these tests can be effective in persuading hesitant students—particularly those with low self-esteem—to participate because the test may indicate unrecognized musical skill. Of course, a poor score certainly should not exclude a student from participation. Use assessments only to report strengths to parents and students in order to encourage instrumental music study. Their purpose for directors is to aid instrument selection in conjunction with other factors, not to dictate it.

Because of time, attention, and cost constraints, this assessment should take as little time as possible for the entire group to complete using paper and pencil. Refer to the test as a "game" to alleviate anxiety, and include practice items so that students as young as eight or nine years old or those with limited English language proficiency easily understand how to "play" it. Rigorous, more precise aptitude tests take more time and materials to administer, but an assessment "game" to aid in instrument selection should be short and simple enough to maintain student interest. The Selmer Music Guidance Survey (Conn-Selmer, n.d.) is an inexpensive assessment that fits these guidelines, though I eliminate a few test questions to save time. Examples of test items (questions) are either recorded on CD or written out so that you can play them on the piano.

Test materials can also come in video form as well. *Band Blast-Off* (Focus on Music, 2008) is an engaging and entertaining recruitment DVD that includes assessments as well as instrument demonstrations and testimonials from actual band students. You can also ask music dealers or colleagues for similar tests.

If on a tight budget, you can use these tests as models to create your own. The Music Achievement Council's (n.d.) "Musical Instrument Game" is no longer available, but has been reprinted with their permission in Table 1.1.

Each section of the Musical Instrument Game consists of six items, which you can quickly score by using an answer key. The first section requires students to indicate if the second of two pitches played on a typical wind instrument is higher, lower, or the same as the first. The second section also requires students to indicate if two groups of four quarter note melodies are the same or different (quarter note = ca 120 beats per minute, 4/4 meter). The third section, which is easiest, requires students to determine if two four-beat rhythm patterns performed on a single pitch using quarter, eighth, and sixteenth note durations are the same or different (quarter note = ca 120 beats per minute, 4/4 meter).

Some scholars encourage directors to select appropriate tests in general based on the degree of reliability, validity, usability, and usefulness (Boyle & Radocy, 1987, p. 154). I have found that tests such as the one mentioned are certainly "usable" in that they are easily administered and "useful" because they suggest which students might progress at about the same rate as other students on instruments requiring certain skills, particularly with wind and percussion instruments.

Table 1.1   Musical Instrument Game

Name					
School					
Classroom Teacher					
Follow instructions and listen carefully					

A. Pitch Recognition

A-1	A-2	A-3	A-4	A-5	A-6
High	High	High	High	High	High
Same	Same	Same	Same	Same	Same
Low	Low	Low	Low	Low	Low

B. Melody Memory

B-1	B-2	B-3	B-4	B-5	B-6
Same	Same	Same	Same	Same	Same
Different	Different	Different	Different	Different	Different

C. Rhythm Memory

C-1	C-2	C-3	C-4	C-5	C-6
Same	Same	Same	Same	Same	Same
Different	Different	Different	Different	Different	Different

© Music Achievement Council. Used with permission.

For example, a score of four to six correct answers on the first section of the Musical Instrument Game and five to six on the second section indicates a student who usually has enough tonal discrimination to discern the close "higher" and "lower" partials on the horn, or to adjust the embouchure naturally in reaction to pitch discrepancies on an oboe. Students who answer only two or three items on the first section but answer the majority of items correctly on the second section are still probably able to discern the high and low pitches needed to negotiate partials on other brass instruments and intonation adjustments on all winds.

Five or six correct answers in the third section requiring rhythm discrimination indicate potential satisfactory progress on some percussion instruments (though versatile percussionists playing timpani and keyboard instruments will need to demonstrate the same skills as other instrumentalists).

All stringed instruments require the same pitch and rhythm abilities, so pitch and rhythm assessments have limited use in predicting instrument success. However, as mentioned earlier, you can use favorable test results to encourage reticent parents and students to participate (Lamb, 1990, p. 142; Hamann & Gillespie, 2004, p. 203).

Though certainly not as precise but necessary due to time constraints, I often must test individual students quickly "on the fly" if they missed the recruiting sessions. We "play" the game quickly; I play examples at the piano, the students answer verbally, and I mark their responses. If really pressed for time, I may modify this further and have them simply match three or four different pitches that I sing. In addition to testing pitch discrimination, I have students echo-clap rhythms while I simultaneously clap a different rhythm to assess students' rhythm memory as well as the independence required to play individual percussion parts.

THE INFORMATION LETTER

Sign-up letters for students to take home should be distributed at the conclusion of the instrument demonstration and skills assessment session. These promotional letters should be as brief, clear, and simply written as possible. They serve to tell parents about the program and specifically describe any commitments, such as after-school rehearsals. Include a section on the form that allows students to indicate instruments that interest them so that you can consider their preferences when deciding on suitable instruments. These information letters should be translated into other languages spoken by families, if necessary. Be sure to have extra copies available and provide students with reminders to bring back forms, such as during morning or afternoon announcements. Students who return a signed information letter are scheduled for a tone production assessment. Figure 1.1 is an example of an information letter I find useful.

Of course, not every child or parent is interested in instrumental music study, and "hard sell" tactics are not necessary or beneficial. But directors can consider contacting parents of students who did not return the sign-up sheet but obtained a high score on assessments given during recruiting to let parents know that their child demonstrates musical ability and might succeed at playing an instrument. I usually call or send home a letter because I believe that students and parents should know about a student's potential success even if the student chooses not to participate. Parents and students are usually pleased to hear such news, and these calls and letters usually add a couple more new students to the roster.

TONE PRODUCTION ASSESSMENT

The fourth component of recruiting allows students to try producing sounds on the instruments. After the deadline for students to return completed forms included in the parental information letter has passed, I schedule students for a tone production assessment. Similar to the initial meeting, I schedule this by classroom. Because of the time involved, only students who have returned the form are assessed. By this time I have the

Anytown Beginning Orchestra or Band
Anytown School
Street Address
City, State 12345
(555) 555-5555
John or Jane Q. Smith, Director

Dear Parent:

Classes are currently being organized for this year's orchestra or band! [A few brief comments about the benefits of instrumental music in general and specific events planned for the year that might generate enthusiasm.] Participation in instrumental music has been linked to academic achievement, as well as many other benefits. But students report that the participation in band or orchestra, though challenging, is also fun!

[Include planned performances or activities here.] We are very excited about the year ahead and are looking forward to winter and spring concerts, as well as our district-wide band or orchestra performance.

All instruction is free and all that is necessary for you to do is rent an instrument from a district-approved music dealer. The school owns a few of the larger band or orchestra instruments students may borrow for the year at no cost.

[Insert any specific program requirements.] If your child begins band or orchestra instruction, he or she must stay for rehearsal one day a week until 3:15. Buses are available to bring students home. Once a week, students have a lesson during the regular school day.

For now, simply complete this form and return it to school by September 3. Information about renting an instrument and other details will be discussed during an information meeting for parents on Thursday, September 25 at 7:00 p.m. in the Anytown Elementary auditorium. Parents should also feel free to call me at Anytown Elementary School (555-5555) on Monday or Tuesday, Anytown Middle School (555-5555) on Wednesday through Friday, or at my home after school hours before 9:00 p.m. at 555-5555.

Yours in music,
John or Jane Q. Smith

Please detach and return to Mr. or Ms. Smith by Sept. 3
Name of Student _____
Instrument:
    1st Choice _____
    2nd Choice _____
    3rd Choice _____
Classroom Teacher This Year:_____
Classroom Teacher Last Year (and school, if different):_____
[Last year's information is helpful if recruiting at the beginning of the school year]
Parent Name: _____
Street Address: _____
City, State Zip: _____
Telephone Day: _____   Evening: _____
Best Time to Call: _____
Parent Signature: _____

Figure 1.1　Informational letter

skills assessment sheets scored and I am ready to use them as guides for discussing instrument suitability.

It is widely purported that some physical characteristics such as lip and teeth structure prohibit satisfactory progress on some instruments. Though true for some pronounced physical barriers (which may be a concern with some exceptional learners), many of these biases have no support (Gordon, 1997, p. 274; Schleuter, 1997, p. 14; Westphal, 1990). However, you can gauge potential success by having students produce sounds on wind instrument mouthpieces or by fingering and bowing stringed instruments. Tone production assessment helps students see firsthand how difficult popular instruments like the flute may be for them or how holding the cello feels more comfortable than the violin, thus promoting balanced instrumentation.

For wind instruments, after an initial demonstration by the director, students should try to produce sounds on a flute head joint and on oboe, clarinet, trumpet, baritone or trombone, and tuba mouthpieces. (Directors should have plenty of sanitizer to use between each student.) Potential flute players can often immediately produce a strong "whistle" on the head joint. It takes a long time to test all students on every type of mouthpiece available in the band, and because of its popularity, controlling the number of saxophonists can be a concern. I have only students who can play the most characteristic and controlled tones on the clarinet mouthpiece also try the saxophone mouthpiece. Though I realize that the two embouchures required are different, I have found that initial success with the clarinet mouthpieces can indicate success on the saxophone mouthpieces.

Students should demonstrate the ability to "buzz" naturally. They usually have "low end" or "high end chops," which is the natural inclination of more (high buzzes or "high end") or less (low buzzes or "low end") lip pressure on the trumpet and trombone, baritone, and euphonium mouthpieces. Students who can buzz in the high range may do well on the trumpet, and those buzzing in the medium to high range can succeed on the horn. "Low end" buzzes indicate future success on the lower brasses. Directors should demonstrate the loose "lip flapping" required for the tuba away from the mouthpiece. Once students can imitate it, they should try to produce a low buzz on the mouthpiece.

Strings require a different tone production assessment. Unlike winds, individual stringed instruments do not require specific musculature for embouchure formation that varies widely between students. It is still very helpful to have students "test drive" instruments as part of the selection process to promote the underrepresented viola, cello, and bass to undecided students.

After students have experienced their initial success with instruments firsthand, directors will find less interest in overrepresented instruments.

Based on the skills assessment, instrument preferences indicated on the sign-up forms, and the tone production assessment, I usually recommend two or three instruments that students may consider. Because students have listed three instrument choices on their sign-up forms, we easily come to an agreement, though students must be happy with this decision. If students (and, in some cases, parents) still insist on a particular instrument, directors can suggest a trial period. Students sometimes surprise the directors with initial success. In other cases, the student realizes—usually within the first two or three weeks—that they should consider another instrument.

After students have tried the instruments, I call every parent with the results. It is important to have two or three choices in mind. Parents, like students, may have gender biases ("The tuba is too big for Sally; how about a more ladylike instrument like the flute?"), preferences based on personal history ("I played the drums, and I think Juan wants to, also"), and instrument partiality due to availability ("Rashonda's older brother used to play the saxophone and we still own one"). Most of the time, however, parents accept the recommendations of the director.

Directors can also extol to parents the financial benefits of playing the underrepresented but often school-owned lower strings and winds. Most importantly, share why you recommend certain instruments with parents, based on the information you collected through the skills and tone production assessments. Even if parents do not follow director recommendations, they see the director as competent and sincerely concerned about both the ensemble and individual students.

The final recruiting session may be a general meeting at night for students, parents, and local music dealers. (Dealers are usually present if purchasing instruments is a requirement.) To avoid damage to instruments, you should instruct dealers to deliver instruments directly to you so that students can demonstrate proper assembly (usually shown at the first lessons) before taking them home.

At the meeting, I give a motivational talk tempered a bit with details about the effort required to meet practice expectations and the commitment necessary to attend rehearsals and performances. If parents cannot make this very brief but important general meeting, calling parents can inform them of important dates, program expectations, and the phone numbers of music dealers so that they can independently make rental arrangements.

ECONOMICALLY DISADVANTAGED SCHOOLS AND STUDENTS

This section has particular relevance for those teaching in schools with significant levels of poverty, especially generational poverty. Payne (2001) defines generational poverty, which is prevalent in many communities, as "having been in poverty for at least two generations; however, the characteristics begin to surface much sooner than two generations if the family lives with others who are from generational poverty. . . . [It] has its own culture, hidden rules, and belief systems" (p. 64). When recruiting urban students, directors may need to consider the importance of entertainment and humor, relationships, matriarchal family structures, and oral language traditions. If such things shape your students' lives, you must be prepared to work within these structures rather than struggle to make students conform to conventional standards.

Less positive characteristics of generational poverty include a belief in fate rather than destiny mitigated by choice, the desire to live in the moment rather than considering future consequences, and lack of organization (Payne, 2001). For underprivileged students, school-owned instruments have tremendous potential to foster responsible behavior while relationships help recruitment.

School-Owned Instruments

Because of widespread poverty, schools in some districts provide most or all instruments for students to borrow, usually with a small rental fee. Philosophically, instrumental music should be offered to every child who wishes to participate. From a pragmatic perspective, there are usually more interested students than available school-owned instruments, so choices often need to be made about who participates, at least at first. Because of instrument shortages, I keep an active waiting list and begin new students throughout the school year.

When assigning school-owned instruments, directors need to consider that not all students should transport instruments to and from school because of dangerous neighborhoods and unstable home environments. Directors can allow students to practice at school as a solution, but home practice is a typical expectation and directors must consider the demonstrated responsibility of students and their families when deciding who borrows an instrument. As a new teacher in an urban school several years ago, I did not account for student responsibility, and I promptly lost three instruments within the first month. To make matters worse, budget constraints prevented replacing them, so fewer students could participate.

The recruiting letter example asks parents or guardians to provide the names of both the current and previous teacher so that directors can confer with classroom teachers about students' demonstrated responsibility. If a teacher gives compelling reasons why a student may not properly care for an instrument, I either make arrangements for students to practice at school or privately share these concerns with the student if I think they can change the behavior. I then put the student on the waiting list to begin later in the year. This way, the student has an opportunity to show the responsible behavior necessary to properly care for an expensive instrument while he or she waits for an available one.

Relationships

Relationships are central for people living in generational poverty because they often provide a way to survive socially and economically. Getting to know students before you recruit them helps to establish a congenial relationship. If students know and like a teacher, that relationship might motivate a student to begin music study more than the activity itself. Students like enthusiastic, personable, and sincere teachers. When communicating with students, teachers should make eye contact and strive to be good listeners. Names mean a lot to students, and teachers should learn them quickly and pronounce them correctly. Directors who show they care about students usually impress them.

To meet and recruit students, directors should make themselves visible by participating in activities outside instrumental music. Directing vocal groups or teaching general music classes makes the director more familiar. For example, as an instrumental music teacher with general music teaching duties for several years, I consistently have several general music students in my instrumental music ensembles. Students get to know and like me in my general music class, and they become interested in joining my instrumental ensembles.

Building relationships with parents is as important as developing them with students, especially for those families living in generational poverty. These parents have many strengths, love their children, and want them to succeed in school as much as more affluent parents. Though gaining parental support is universally important across settings, directors can adopt strategies designed specifically for particular socioeconomic demographics.

Parents living in poverty want their children to do well in school, but they often don't know how to negotiate school organizational structures or may have animosity towards schools based on their own negative experiences. Though parents may view school unfavorably, they, like their children, support teachers they like. If directors want parental support, they must strive to make contact with parents or guardians of prospective students during the recruiting process using the same interpersonal skills they use to recruit students.

Parent contact may take more effort in some cases. Sometimes families do not have phones, and directors must visit homes to discuss recruiting information. In other cases, parents may not speak English. Fortunately, students can often translate, and school personnel and community members may know the language. Software programs can translate recruiting letters into common languages such as Spanish (though someone fluent must proofread them, since these translations are often imprecise).

True, cases exist where the lack of parental concern is heartbreaking—and this neglect is not exclusive to underserved students in disadvantaged schools. But with some tenacity, the director can get strong support early in the recruiting stage from most parents, greatly aiding student success by encouraging practicing at home, attending performances, and meeting other program expectations.

A well-planned, diligent approach to recruiting students establishes a strong foundation for your instrumental music program. Carefully matching students with appropriate instruments and encouraging the participation of parents and family members sets up your music students for long-term success.

Two

Maintaining Interest

Retention practices across all teaching environments generally have far more similarities than differences. Instruction that motivates students has similar power in suburban, rural, and urban schools, but directors may need to modify some techniques because of local economic conditions or cultures. Committed directors can foster success and motivate students to continue instrumental music study regardless of teaching and learning environments.

Successful recruiting is of little significance if directors do not make an effort to retain students once they have begun study. Current trends in scheduling, mandatory testing, and other issues have led to widespread instrumental program attrition in general, and many of these weighty issues require a degree of advocacy beyond the scope of this book. The current discussion centers on retaining students from a structural and instructional perspective, from within the instrumental music program itself.

After the excitement of learning a new instrument wears off, the reality of home practice takes its place. Dropout rates of up to one-third of the original recruiting number are not unusual between the first and second year of beginner programs. In a study of orchestra programs, Hamann, Gillespie, and Bergonzi (2002, as cited in Hamann & Gillespie, 2004, p. 208) report a national average retention rate (students staying in the program) of 73 percent between the first and second year, another 73 percent between elementary and middle or junior high school, and yet another 73 percent retention rate between middle or junior high school and high school with a total retention rate of 53 percent of students from beginner program to high school. The total attrition rate equals 47 percent of students.

This rate reflects the approximate retention average in my beginning ensembles, though I structure my program so I can replace these students with new ones throughout most of the school year. Nonetheless, this percentage rate presents an alarming amount of attrition for some directors, particularly if their programs do not have revolving enrollment and recruitment numbers are low to begin with. Administrators, parents, and other district instrumental music teachers closely scrutinize numbers to assess program justification in the elementary schools, projected strength in the higher grades, and director competence.

A certain amount of attrition is unavoidable, but large attrition numbers can be kept to a minimum when as many students as possible have the opportunity to participate and when directors pay proper attention to providing every student with motivating and meaningful experiences.

The large numbers desired when recruiting are necessary, in part, to account for the inevitable dropout of some students. A study by Boyle, DeCarbo, and Jordan (1995) describes causes of attrition:

> Loss of interest by students is the most cited factor that affects participation. Other major factors that have been reported include lack of communication, interest in participation in other activities and sports, and class scheduling conflicts. Financial concerns, although cited, generally was not a factor in determining participation in instrumental music programs. (p. 2)

The research suggests that some factors exist beyond directors' immediate control, but it also shows what they can address. When multiple activities vie for students' time, not all students share the necessary commitment to learn an instrument. Directors can keep students in the program by discussing the reasons for waning interest and seeking to find solutions. They can consult other teachers or administrators about scheduling conflicts. Parents can illuminate problems that students may be too timid to discuss with the director.

Strategies that motivate students and improve retention may require an examination of program structure as well as instruction. As a teacher, you must have clear expectations and strive to be firm but fair—and even likable! Work to keep students engaged by monitoring rehearsal pace, and include games and game-like activities to add interest. Perform often, provide meaningful feedback often, and communicate often with parents. You have to keep a lot of balls in the air at once, but your students—and their continued interest—will reward you.

TWO PROGRAM STRUCTURE SOLUTIONS

Directors may need to consider program policy structure and instruction in their efforts to reduce attrition. Some directors mistakenly believe that they must retain all students, regardless of demonstrated commitment, because program merit is assessed solely on ensemble numbers. Other directors feel that some students' interest and commitment "blossoms" with maturity, and they encourage them to continue, even without ample home practice, lesson attendance, or other typical expectations. It takes only one or two uncommitted students to make even a large ensemble sound poor, though, and many uncommitted students only make it worse.

Ensemble quality is important even to young students, particularly those who believe that high performance quality is a goal of study. All students must bear the burden of having unprepared students in the ensemble. It is often not the few unprepared students who are most frustrated, but the more motivated students in the ensemble. These motivated students may quit and join other ensembles, pursue musical experiences as soloists, or much worse, discontinue instrumental music study altogether.

Some programs have the benefit of both small-group instruction or "lessons" (typically using the "pull-out" system where students miss portions of other classes, usually on a rotation schedule) and large-group instruction or rehearsals. To avoid a large disparity in skill level, directors might require students to demonstrate prerequisite skills to participate in the full ensemble. Benchmarks for participation keep the pace of success rewarding for students. Clearly explain requirements, assess them objectively, and report progress to parents and students.

Students who do not demonstrate the necessary prerequisite skills may not participate in the full ensemble until they are proficient. Encourage them to continue their music study, but they may need individual lessons because those in group lessons are further ahead. The present discussion involves typical students who struggle because of a lack of practice, attendance, or motivation to fulfill other program requirements; a detailed discussion of modifications for exceptional students will take place in Chapter 6.

In many cases, individual instruction without ensemble participation does not retain students because they sense they are atypical, and ensemble participation usually works as a powerful motivator for continued study. Some struggling students become more motivated and responsible enough to practice and fulfill other expectations when they get a bit older. Rather than allowing them to quit permanently because of a temporary maturity, encourage them to start later.

My first-year groups are open to fourth and fifth graders, and I have a second-year, more advanced group that consists primarily of fifth graders (though the actual grade levels vary depending on program structure in other schools). Because fourth graders typically move at a slower pace, the older fifth-grade beginners can both begin an instrument and acquire most of the skills of the second-year fifth graders by year's end. This accelerated pace is an expectation at the outset, and the older beginners are usually motivated to catch up to their peers.

The multi-grade beginner option allows students who were not successful in one grade to try again a year later, often with noteworthy success. It may be useful in programs that do not have schedules that allow students to catch up in small-group or individual instruction. Multi-grade structure also permits new students moving from schools where programs began at different ages (for example, all beginners started in fifth grade instead of fourth grade) to join.

I have had some struggling students "repeat" a year in the first-year groups, particularly when their friends or relatives either began as fifth graders or repeated the year with them (so they had a buddy). Rather than having some students complete and then repeat a second year, it might be better to have them discontinue study and resume the next school year. Starting beginners in more than one grade may not be possible in all programs, but can be an option when trying to decrease attrition while maintaining adequate ensemble progress.

TEACHER DEMEANOR AND EXPECTATIONS

Teacher demeanor is as important for retaining students as it is for recruiting them. (Additionally, see Chapter 4 for discussion about how teacher demeanor is important to student management.) Some directors misinterpret "positive demeanor" and adopt the saccharin persona of a children's television show host. Directors do not need to be excessively sweet to be effective, even with young students. If they are enthusiastic—indeed, passionate—about teaching music and are "hip" to the given age group, they usually inspire and engage students.

Instrumental music study requires effort, and students tolerate and even expect a consistent and objective director who insists that students meet high expectations. In my experience, students often describe these teachers as "strict," but not "mean." "Mean" teachers demonstrate sarcasm, spite, inequity, and other indications of animosity toward some or all children. "Strict" teachers have expectations for students and ensemble quality and are consistent in reaching those goals.

AVOIDING BOREDOM

Fortunately, playing an instrument is inherently engaging, but overly long periods of teacher-talk, working with individual sections, or managing behavior restricts playing time and invites boredom. Directors should plan thoroughly to keep things moving, but plans must be abandoned if they are not working. Whenever I do not complete objectives for the sake of optimal pacing, I note unfulfilled objectives in my lesson plan so they can be included in future classes.

Understanding or mastering the "stuff"—content, concepts, and skills—of instrumental music study is often just plain work. But work in the form of play constitutes the single most powerful approach I can recommend for meaningfully engaging students. To be considered instruction rather than recreation, these games must have very clear objectives and assessments to monitor attainment of objectives.

Given limited instruction time, games should not take too long, have complex rules, or require several materials. Games can be the same as those familiar to students, or be game-like activities, meaning tasks structured in the manner in which children play (see below for an example). They effectively introduce, reinforce, review, or assess.

Learning activities modeled after familiar children's and sports games provide engaging contexts. In Chapter 4, I detail how these games can be used in classroom management systems. Instrumental music educator Steve Frank of West Genesee Central School District in Camillus, New York, contributed the following "Video Baseball." It has student appeal, and achieves and assesses a specific goal: accuracy in reading music notation.

> In order to play "Video Baseball," identify performance material, such as short passages groups can use that also contain "tricky" situations that truly test reading ability.
>
> I use a baseball format for this "video game," but the game can be easily adapted. In this version, the students receive a certain number of "at bats," based on the difficulty of material or available time. Each student takes a turn playing one line of music at a time. For example, the first student attempts a perfect performance of line 1 and if he or she plays it correctly the first time, the student earns an extra "at bat." Students earn an extra "at bat" only if they play the line correctly during the first attempt. A correct performance on the second or third attempt allows them only to proceed to the next line of material.
>
> If a mistake is made, the student is "honked" immediately upon making the mistake. (I make a sound resembling the buzzer used at athletic events.) "Honking" the mistake immediately allows students to know where they made a mistake and they can immediately check to see what they did wrong. When a student "strikes out," I "honk" to signal the mistake while signaling "out" by thrusting my thumb upwards (imitating a baseball umpire). Imitating a mechanical computer-generated voice, I say, "game over." The kids love this part. . . .
>
> Students can't advance through the material until they play the line correctly or "strike out" trying. Play continues, alternating from student to student, through the designated material until everyone has played everything or has "struck out" trying. Everyone can be a winner—anyone who stays "at bat" up to the end of the material wins.

Students of all ages find games like this one motivating, provided that the games are modified for specific age levels. Due to the proliferation of mature video games with violent themes, consider benign contexts such as sports-oriented "video games."

It is quite possible that the same students will consistently win the music reading game because they are naturally more skilled notation decoders. And no one enjoys the game when the same people win (except the winners, of course). Students have different strengths; using games for other skills such as intonation, breathing, or expression will likely produce multiple winners. If competitive elements in games cause concern, structuring games that require teamwork can reduce competition and encourage students—particularly those who are struggling.

Game-like activities draw from children's play experiences but lack the structure required for games. For example, after students learn proper breathing technique and have had opportunities to practice it, directors can engage students with this challenge: "Let's see if we can all 'sizzle' (or 'hiss,' which is similar to breathing required for wind instruments) for ten seconds." After correcting any breathing errors, directors can challenge all students to "sizzle" for 15 seconds, then 20 seconds, and so on, correcting breathing errors after each challenge. The goal is demonstrating proper breathing technique away from the instrument; assessment comes from teacher and student observation. The activity, presented as a contest, de-emphasizes competition as all students breathe together; no student gets singled out for scrutiny and there are no individual winners.

For game ideas, resources such as *Teaching Techniques and Insights for Instrumental Music Educators* (Casey, 1993) and *Band Rehearsal Techniques: A Handbook for New Directors* (Dalby, 1993) devote entire sections to games. Directors can adapt age-appropriate and relevant board games and video games. The possibilities are limitless, and playful activities that have clear goals and assessment have great instructional and motivational power.

PERFORMING

I still remember terse advice prominently posted in a university computer cluster that read "Save Early. Save Often." Conspicuously posted because of the many incidences of losing crucial data, this advice has equal import with respect to students if it reads "Perform Early. Perform Often." Like games, performing motivates and prevents students from losing the important material they have mastered. Because the motivational benefit of performance wanes within a couple of weeks, schedule more than just the perfunctory winter and spring concerts. Performances need not be formal like those in winter and spring; they may only involve playing a segment or entire piece in front of the principal, teacher, or group of students. Soloists, a few students in a lesson group, or the entire ensemble can perform. These informal "concerts" help minimize performance anxiety, and I include as many of these impromptu performances as I can when preparing students for solo and ensemble festivals.

PRAISE, FEEDBACK, AND PUBLIC RECOGNITION

Kohn (1999) and others have denounced praise and other rewards as ineffective, even harmful, in motivating students. One of their central arguments is that motivation should be intrinsic, or self-generated, rather than extrinsic, or based on teacher approval or tangible rewards like food. There are sound reasons for this argument. However, many district- or school-wide student management systems are still based on extrinsic rewards. If instrumental music teachers decide to implement systems counter to those instituted in the school, they are at odds with colleagues and administration. Further, consistency is a key component of any management system and should be in place in all classrooms. And although I no longer advocate harmful bribery such as junk food or candy rewards, I still believe rewards that are linked to learning goals can be structured so that they are not harmful or ineffective.

"What constitutes reward?—That which the student will work toward" (Madsen & Madsen, 1983, p. 54). Madsen and Madsen further identify words (spoken and written), expressions (facial and bodily), closeness (nearness and touching, though touching obviously is not recommended in today's schools), activities and privilege (social and individual), and things (tokens, food, playthings, money) as the types of rewards children work toward (1983, p. 59).

Whether you agree with the benefits of these types of rewards or not, students respond much better to positive techniques of reinforcement rather than negative ones of disapproval or punishment, as Madsen and Madsen crucially observe (1983, p. 59). The following strategies are for using verbal reinforcement and public recognition effectively because of their shared power in retaining and instructing all students through motivation.

Though Kohn (1999) and others do not endorse its use, teacher approval communicated through verbal praise is rewarding to most students. Praise can bolster students' feelings of competence of self-efficacy, which some research suggests plays a role in prolonged music study (O'Neill & McPherson, 2002, Chap. 3). However, given many experts' opposition to extrinsic rewards such as praise, and the fact that many students may react negatively to public recognition in class by the teacher, I temper verbal praise and make recognition less a reflection of my approval and more focused on the actions or behavior of students.

This positive verbal feedback must be clear and specific in order to motivate and instruct the student. Other students present learn vicariously and work toward acheiving the same goal. Vague, nonspecific feedback, even if genuine, is ineffective because students do not know what to work toward. Thus, "Great, cellos!" rewards cello students, but "Cellos, you kept your bows parallel to the bridge throughout the entire passage" is specific enough to be instructive, is not a reflection of the teacher's approval, and focuses on the proper technique students demonstrate. Further, it instructs the whole class so that all can work toward proper bow angle. Skillful use of this type of specific feedback saves rehearsal time because the director gives instruction and reinforcement at the same time.

Although I tend to avoid a good deal of value-laden teacher praise, I do endorse other types of public recognition of achievement. Some students earn special recognition for activities, such as regional honor groups, but these exemplary students do not make up the entire ensemble, and every member needs an opportunity for recognition. Announcing "Band or Orchestra Student(s) of the Week" during morning or afternoon announcements is effective for elementary students, and is instructive if students know the criteria for selection. Though exemplary students may earn this distinction during the first few weeks, other students should receive the award for achievements, such as an outstanding lesson or display of citizenship, so that as many students are rewarded as possible by the end of the year.

You can display achievement posters in prominent locations in the school to motivate students of all ages (though you might need to adjust the "coolness" factor for middle and high school students). Students sign their names on the posters as they earn predetermined goals for each level, such as a specific number of parent-signed practice records or successful performance of a passage or entire piece.

Individualize goals to increase success rates. For example, one student might earn their signature on the Achievement Level 1 poster for successful completion of an étude, while another student reaches the same level for two consecutive weeks of prompt and prepared lesson attendance. Students sign the posters themselves after fulfilling predetermined requirements, and each level can bring additional recognition of some sort, like a ribbon, a note home, and so on. In schools with bilingual students, achievement level posters can be written in all represented languages.

Students aim to arrive at all achievement levels by the end of the school year, and I find that ten levels work well for this length of time. Although older students often act ambivalent about the recognition system, I see that the achievement level display is a necessary stop for students of all ages when visiting the school with their parents. Again, clearly communicated criteria for the various levels can simultaneously motivate and instruct students.

PARENTS

Positive communication that builds bridges to parents is vital for keeping students in ensembles. Despite the best efforts of directors to motivate students, their interest has peaks and valleys. Parents can encourage students through those valleys of low interest, and a strong partnership between director and parents is often the key to helping students through them. Sharing students' success either by phone, note, or in person helps to build necessary parent partnerships that retains students.

CONSIDERING STUDENTS LIVING IN POVERTY AND DIVERSE CULTURES

Revolving enrollment, practicing, and competition have particular import when trying to decrease dropout rates of students living in poverty. Consider learning styles, competition, and culturally relevant music to retain students from diverse cultures.

Revolving Enrollment

In order to keep numbers up in schools with high levels of student poverty, particularly if you have more interested students than school-owned instruments available, directors may need to start students throughout most of the school year as instruments become available. During the last third of the year, students may simply take individual or small group lessons in preparation for the following year.

Remember that ensemble participation with peers is important to students and a key factor in retaining them, so they need to participate in rehearsals as soon as possible. Directors can reward student effort by phasing in participation. For example, a goal to learn all or merely a part of the easiest piece the ensemble is currently preparing can serve as a condition of participation for the new student. The part can even be simplified at first. Expect that the new student will continue to work to catch up to the ensemble as the year progresses.

Programs that don't have "lessons" can phase students in gradually, but students simply cannot play during pieces or passages they do not know. Although they want to learn pieces quickly so they can play more during rehearsal, directors should realize that students new to the ensemble can feel overwhelmed by the advanced skill level of peers. Clearly defined, individualized, incremental goals help encourage new students.

Peer tutors can help students catch up. This strategy helps the tutee, but also challenges the tutors as they draw on more advanced thinking skills by teaching the material (Kaplan & Stauffer, 1994). Directors can assign new students to a competent peer to help during rehearsals, lessons, and even practice at home. With students who are learning English, consider tutors who can also serve as translators.

Practicing

Some students may live in dangerous neighborhoods, have neighbors or family members who complain about noise, or are not allowed to transport large instruments on crowded buses. Practicing at school may be an option for students who cannot practice regularly or at all at home or who cannot transport instruments to and from school. I converted a storage area within view of the music room for this purpose. Students can practice during, before, or after school hours. Students who must practice at school have the benefit of added guidance from the director, so the practice sessions are usually very effective. Practicing at school for as little as 20 minutes every other day can be the deciding factor in keeping a student progressing at a pace necessary to stay in the instrumental music program.

Cultural Learning Styles

The learning styles increasingly represented in economically disadvantaged schools suggest that planning instruction that motivates students helps to decrease dropout rates. Scholars describe ideal African American learning experiences as relevant, purposeful, social, and offering high degrees of stimulation (Hale, 2001; Kunjufu, 1986, 1990, 2002). Through my experiences in urban and rural schools, I have found that teaching practices to account for cultural learning style characteristics posited by these scholars work well with students in general. Though playing an instrument addresses many of these learning needs inherently, teachers need to plan instruction that ensures ample playing time as well as similarly engaging experiences, like singing, during those brief periods when students do not play.

Competition

Warily approach the dynamics of competition and cooperation. "Some cultures highly value group success and therefore encourage cooperative behavior over competitive behavior" (Colarusso & O'Rourke, 2004, p. 19).

In other instances, children from generational poverty often lack skills necessary to mediate behavior, especially in competitive environments. They may have experienced little success in school and give up easily with the perception of failure. To respect certain cultural perspectives, avoid peer conflicts, build a sense of esprit de corps, and keep perceived failure at a minimum, directors should consider activities that reward students for group achievements. Structuring activities for group success accounts for the social learning styles ascribed to some cultures, and it helps all students positively perceive success.

Cultural Relevancy

A rich diversity of cultures exists in some schools. Students like to play musical styles that reflect their own cultures, though culturally relevant music should not be the only music they learn, as it is our responsibility to teach students about as much of the world's various music styles as possible. Unfortunately, much of the band and orchestra music available is Eurocentric and may not motivate students because of its unfamiliarity. Older students in particular tend to have trouble staying motivated when they play only Western-styled music. Danny Lopez, an urban instrumental music teacher in Texas, offers a compelling rationale for culturally relevant ensembles by describing his own experiences:

> All my kids have probably seen mariachi from the time they were small. In San Antonio, it's traditional at every wedding to have a mariachi. You really don't see bands that often unless you go to a high school football game or a college football game—and my kids ordinarily don't go to college football games or concerts. . . . My kids don't know a lot of the folk songs in the beginning band books. They're inner-city people and they don't know "Go Tell Aunt Rhody". . . . [Y]ou've got to start with "their" music. You've got to find out what kids are listening to, and then use that music in class. (Taylor, Barry, & Walls, 1997, pp. 69–70)

The type of culturally relevant music differs based on geographic area or student ethnicity and may be unfamiliar to directors. In the case of mariachi, band and orchestra instruments are used (with the addition of guitars or voice), but other culturally relevant ensembles may require nontraditional instruments. A growing number of printed and recorded resources for teaching these ensembles have become available. Directors can immerse themselves more fully in a musical style by attending workshops and clinics (see Music, 2009 for specific culturally relevant music examples and resources).

Such instrumental ensembles sometimes exist in schools as extracurricular activities. Volunteers often teach them, and ensembles tend to focus on entertainment value rather than the serious study of authentic performance. This should not be the case if a certified music teacher is available. Directors must remember that these ensembles, like traditional bands and orchestras, have a standard of performance quality and can conform to national, state, and district standards. *Strategies for Teaching Specialized Ensembles*, edited by Robert A. Cutietta (1999), provides an excellent resource to help directors align alternative ensembles with music standards. These ensembles are as legitimate as traditional ones, and directors should strive to provide motivating, substantive music experiences that also reflect students' cultures.

Traditional bands and orchestras should play culturally relevant music as well. Much of the so-called multicultural music in the past merely constituted arrangements of folk material from different parts of Europe. Fortunately, a growing number of pieces at all skill levels have become available that more authentically reflect world music styles. Just as you can support a weak or nonexistent bass or other section by adding a synthesizer to the ensemble, you can also expand instrumentation to increase authenticity. For example, add instruments such as djembe, conga, or claves to African or Latin folk arrangements; guitar, vihuela, or guitarron to string orchestra mariachi arrangements; or mandolins or guitars to fiddle arrangements. You can introduce students to instrumental music study by using the cultural music with which they identify, but they should perform varied music from all over the world. Substantive music originates from all cultures.

If directors cannot find or afford world music literature, they can arrange pieces in a given music style themselves. Given the limited budgets of economically disadvantaged schools, this may be a necessity. These arrangements do not need to be complex; writing a simple unison melody often suffices for beginners. As dictated by the style of music, arrangements for older students may need the addition of harmony, bass line, and percussion parts. Whether performing published pieces or arrangements written by the director, students find "their" music motivating to play, and audiences usually respond enthusiastically.

Student retention depends on many factors, some of which you can control and others you can't. Put your energy into inspiring students to achieve high standards by implementing classroom policies that motivate, engage, and, ultimately, retain.

Three

Gaining Support

Because funding for instrumental music programs often gets called into question, directors need to search continually for ideas that publicize their program's achievements and elevate their prominence. You can do many things to inform parents, administrators, and other stakeholders about the viability of instrumental music programs. Directors who establish good public relations celebrate student achievement and successfully build support for programs.

PARENTS

As an inexperienced teacher several years ago, I was uneasy with parents in general and nearly terrified of a few of them in particular. I was not prepared for the power that parents could wield. Through the advice of mentors and doing a good bit of reading and reflection on my own, I learned that parents are powerful allies, but I would have to enlist their support proactively. I have since improved my rapport with parents a good deal. In fact, I have built programs in some otherwise adverse conditions through parental support and subsequent administrative support.

Early and frequent communication with parents provides a sense of legitimacy. Large numbers of students are typically involved in the instrumental music program, so their parents create a powerful force that can preserve program vitality in the face of scheduling and funding crises.

Though often quite strong in elementary schools, frequent communication with parents wanes with the increasing age of the student. Maturing students press for autonomy and independence, especially in the middle and high school years. Though they do not object to peripheral involvements such as fund-raising, students expect less overt involvement from parents, particularly at school. However, older children still seek the approval of parents, who continue to affect their children's success no matter what their age.

Assessment reporting provides a simple yet crucial way to keep parents informed of their child's progress and program expectations. Grades or other assessments provide effective communication if they accurately and objectively identify students' strengths as well as areas for improvement. A program with clear, identifiable, and measurable goals communicates the academic legitimacy of instrumental music study. Brophy (2000) argues, "When music teachers are armed with assessment data that demonstrate learning and student progress toward attaining educational standards, their programs are much more supportable when districts face budget cuts" (p. 2). Students, in turn, find favorable assessments rewarding. Assessment has vital importance for both instruction and advocacy.

As the director, you need to initiate relationships with parents—a difficult task. Written announcements that detail upcoming events are necessary forms of communication, but these are impersonal. The director talks to parents during functions at school, but there are usually too many parents to greet in a short amount of time.

Phone calls present opportunities to discuss student progress while building personal rapport. It is best to call parents when they are free to talk, so ask what time of day is most convenient to receive calls when collecting phone numbers. Even if parents are not home, you can leave brief messages such as a congratulatory note about a good lesson or other praise. In my experience, some parents have trouble contacting me at school. In all correspondence, I have chosen to provide my home number. You may want to consider giving out an e-mail address, but most of my students' parents don't have computers (and I didn't have one at school until recently).

I have never had problems with giving out my home phone number in any school in which I have taught, even in newsletters. The advent of caller ID has virtually ended prank phone calling, though I tell students clearly that my phone number is for parent use (as friendly students merely wanting to chat have called in the past!). Of course, not everyone should give out e-mail and home phone numbers. In many cases, directors manage large programs and might become inundated with work-related issues if dealing with calls and e-mails when they—and their families—need the time away from work.

I try to speak personally to parents at least three times a year. Sometimes these conferences are congratulatory phone calls and merely let parents know that their child is doing well. These phone calls reward students powerfully. They excitedly tell me how happy their parents were to receive good news. Even if I call with a problem, I find one or two student strengths to share with parents to temper the tone of the call.

In all direct communication with parents, directors must communicate problems concerning student progress precisely and objectively. For example, instead of vague language and details such as, "C. J. is doing poorly," directors should use objective language supported by evidence: "The last two lessons, C. J. could not keep up with the rest of the group and seemed unfamiliar with pieces on page ten. I spoke to him privately after both lessons and he told me he was having a hard time practicing at home. I don't want him to fall behind. How can we work together to solve this?"

Directors should also listen carefully to parents and acknowledge their feelings, validate their concerns, and check for understanding by asking questions such as, "It is clear to me that you are frustrated. If I understand you correctly, you are upset that Shahadah is being treated unfairly, right? Well, I am glad that we have this opportunity to talk about it." Please note that directors should never have to endure verbal abuse or insults, and they should end conversations that take this course. But directors should try to understand feelings and arrive at solutions, even during those unpleasant phone calls where parents become upset. Experience has shown that such frustration usually results from lack of communication, and I have fewer of these types of calls as my efforts to communicate with parents improve each year. I have come a long way since my first couple of years of teaching!

Even when students drop from the program, I make sure I call parents to thank them for their support and to ensure that no one has any hard feelings. Even before I get around to calling, some parents call or write on their own to explain that their children's discontinuation of study was not my fault and to thank me for my efforts. Even though their child is no longer in the program, these parents remain ardent supporters and encourage participation with younger family members or friends.

To effectively communicate and build support, directors need to understand local cultures and values. Directors often do not come from the communities in which they teach and may have different values and perspectives, encountering "oppositional frames of reference" (Ogbu, 1992, p. 9), particularly if the director is white or another ethnicity not largely represented in the community. These different frames of reference may exist because of history, socioeconomics, ethnicity, and geographic location. Directors can talk to veteran teachers in the district, read articles and books written by experts on certain cultures and communities, and be sensitive to different perspectives by carefully observing students, parents, and community members.

Numerous resources discuss successful parent–teacher conferencing, active listening, and other effective communication techniques that help you get along well with parents as well as colleagues, administrators, and students. Though frequent, individual communication with parents is time consuming in large ensembles, the relationships that you develop generate great support for the ensemble—something well worth the effort. Some of the most powerful feedback administrators receive about your program comes from parents; the more parents who provide feedback, the more powerful the message.

Parental support has as much importance in economically disadvantaged schools as it does in affluent schools. Many teachers, particularly if they view family structure through a white, middle-class perspective, criticize and underestimate the parental support of their students. Realize, however, that students of diverse ethnicity or students living in poorer communities may have extremely strong familial bonds. Kuykendall (1992) points out that "some [teachers] would be surprised to learn of the tremendous strength that exists in non-nuclear, but 'extended' Black and Hispanic families" (p. 98).

Other researchers promote extended family support, but they also underscore the impact parents themselves can have on students' efforts at school. A study by Wilson and Corbett (2001) sought to ascertain what type of teachers urban middle school students prefer, and their statements are illuminating:

> [Interviewer]: Why are you getting an A in reading when you did so poorly last year?
> [Student 1]: I work hard. She's [the teacher] hard on us. I like that. It's helping me.
> [Researcher]: What does she do?
> [Student 1]: She called my house and talked to my mom.
> [Student 2]: A teacher who stays on you is one who tells you to do your work, calls your house over and over and over, says "You're missing this and that" and "You need to turn this in."
> [Researcher]: What do your best teachers do to help you the most?
> [Student 3]: She knows my mom real good. She stays on my back. She says she'll call my mom. (p. 72)

In their own words, these students show how much power parents and teachers have, especially when combined, in molding student behavior.

Some parents distrust teachers and act generally hostile toward school representatives because of bad experiences they or their children had or cultural differences that language barriers possibly heightened. They may not place the same value on education as teachers do. But directors must realize that these parents will develop positive relationships with teachers they like and trust; building bridges to ambivalent parents is possible.

Contacting parents can be more challenging in areas with high levels of poverty. Because many of these parents can find only low-paying jobs, they often need to work several hours beyond the average work week, often with varied schedules. In these cases, students often stay with extended family or friends during evening hours. Many families living in poverty are grappling with day-to-day survival. They might fear phone calls from school only bring more bad news, so perhaps they screen them.

When families do not have access to phones, I ask students for phone numbers of other family members. I also frequently mail home congratulatory notes. Thus, I make some of my parent contact by leaving messages with family members or on answering machines. As with speaking to parents directly, these messages always include positive comments about the student. Although I share positive comments freely, I save any areas of concern for discussion directly with the parent. In some cases, if I understand the particular family dynamics well enough, I'll discuss these concerns with extended family members as well.

HOME VISITS

Many teachers equate family involvement with presence at school functions such as parent–teacher conferences and open houses held during evening hours. However, Payne (2006) offers the following advice:

> Do not confuse having physical presence with parental involvement. The research seems to indicate that when a parent provides *support, insistence,* and *expectations* to the child, the presence or absence of a parent in the physical school building is immaterial. Therefore, [communication with] parents should concentrate on these issues. (p. 1)

It is indisputable that support from parents is critical with student success. Insistence from parents for students to practice at home is integral to success in instrumental music. Further, expectations such as attending performances and dress requirements are also important. Many parents will be informed and educated about these types of support merely through traditional letters from teachers and periodic meetings at schools.

As mentioned earlier, many families do not receive or understand newsletters or cannot or will not attend functions at school. In order to work with all families, home visits are the single most important strategy you can employ to garner support from home. Unfortunately, it is most often lacking when working with underserved students and their families. If families are not present at school, take information to them.

I try to visit homes as often as possible because these visits are usually very positive and successful in garnering family support, but directors need to judge whether or not it is safe to visit homes alone in some environments. (And if you think it is dangerous for you, imagine what it is like for a child to walk to and from school every day!) Some teachers make home visits with other teachers, while others bring spouses. Be sure to check with your building principal and ascertain if there are school or district policies about home visits.

Treat visits as you would meetings at school. Disseminate information and expectations, including performance dates and classroom behavior plans. If students have missed rehearsals or lessons at school, I will give lessons in their homes, though I always make sure an adult is present by scheduling these lessons ahead of time. Parents and other family members are fascinated with these lessons, as they see the academic side to music making. They are also proud to see their child learning how to play a real musical instrument and experience success he or she may not achieve in other academic areas. Families also see the teacher as especially dedicated and come to respect them as a result of the visit. Though some families resist getting to know me no matter what, working to secure support from all families regardless of socioeconomic condition is central to building and maintaining a healthy instrumental music program.

ADMINISTRATORS AND COLLEAGUES

Parental support is a powerful ally in maintaining an instrumental music program, but building administrators often make the decisions that determine your program's fate. Principals must often manage near the bottom of the power structure in a top-down bureaucracy. Regardless of district size or structure, government mandates frequently determine the decisions administrators must make. However, recent widespread adoption of site-based management models often allows building principals autonomy in scheduling, building use, and funding allocations. In many instances, administrators—including building principals—can either crush or cultivate instrumental music programs. It's best to have them on your side.

Keeping administrators aware of instrumental program events and achievements reminds them that your program is vibrant and vital. Administrators can reward and encourage students by sharing program achievements through building announcements and conversations with the students themselves. Recognition from people in positions of authority are quite motivating for students.

Similar to administrators, developing relationships with fellow teachers can enhance both your job and your program. Teaching with other colleagues increases visibility and builds collegial bonds that often lead to support of the instrumental music ensemble. Collegial partnering can be as simple as having science students come to the music room for a demonstration of sympathetic vibrations for a few minutes, or as involved as an entire unit on Shakespeare's *Romeo and Juliet* and its contemporary adaptation, *West Side Story*. Even nonacademic support, like volunteering the music room for certain students who need time out or covering another teacher's classroom for a bathroom break, helps garner their support.

Publicize your program's events as much as possible. Distribute announcements about upcoming performances to administrators, as well as news about success meeting standards and other curricular developments typically sent home to parents. Principals usually require that you submit these notices to them for approval before distribution to parents. Even if your school does not have this policy, you should submit any correspondence for distribution outside school to principals first to keep them in the loop. Besides program achievements, keep them informed regarding program needs and issues concerning scheduling, instructional space, and budget.

One-on-one conversations provide an obvious opportunity to promote your program. When directors must pose problems to the administrator, they can posit two or more viable solutions if possible. Because problems presented by new teachers may be viewed as insignificant or a result of inexperience, new teachers can consider having an experienced colleague participate in the discussion. The presence of supportive colleagues shows that you have productive relationships with other staff members—a critical assessment component in many teacher evaluations.

Skillful and competent administrators judiciously weigh instrumental program needs along with other numerous considerations. Unfortunately, the weight assigned often correlates to the value administrators place on music and the arts in general. Savvy administrators who do not personally value instrumental music still work to cultivate and maintain healthy programs if parents and other community members strongly support the program.

Build support by including administrators in performances. Most principals enjoy being on stage as much as students do! Have them serve as narrators or even as performers. "First Performance: A Demonstration Concert" for band (Feldstein, 2000) and orchestra (Feldstein, 1994), a chart distributed by the Music Achievement Council, constitutes a performance that requires a narrator. My building principal enthusiastically accepts my invitation every year. I recently wrote a beginning band piece integrated with English or language arts classes that included vignettes performed by building administrators and other teachers. Students feel important when they perform with administrators, and the performance itself provides an opportunity for administrators to display their support for instrumental music programs.

COMMUNITY AWARENESS

Though sharing program achievements with parents and administrators constitutes a form of publicity, directors must make the greater community aware of program vitality. Announcements of community interest include performances, honors and awards, and professional accomplishments of the director. Greater publicity motivates students because it recognizes their achievements to others outside school. Parents and administrators appreciate the community notices the program, in turn strengthening their support. Figure 3.1 is a press release template appropriate for announcing instrumental music concerts.

In addition to program achievements and events, directors should consider announcing their own professional development and accomplishments. Publicity of such announcements depends on the size of the community and the targeted readership or audience of the media outlet. If published or broadcast, these announcements strengthen the instrumental music program by showing that it has a skilled director committed to further training and service to the profession. From a motivational perspective, students take pride in a director who has acknowledged achievements, and they need not be extraordinary. Figure 3.2 is a press release template provided by MENC, which should be printed on school letterhead.

Press Release
For release: [date]
Contact:

LOCAL ORCHESTRA PERFORMS CONCERT

The [name] School Orchestra will give a free concert of [day of the week], [date], at [time] in the school auditorium.

[Name of director], a music educator at [school], will conduct the orchestra in the performance, which will feature both popular and traditional selections.

For more information about the concert, call [name and phone].

Figure 3.1   Press release template

Press Release
For more information, contact: [Your name] at [your phone number]
For Immediate Release

[Your Name] Returns from Attending
Prestigious Music Education Conference in Bellevue, Washington

[Date of Release] [Your city, state]—[Your name] recently returned to class at [your school] after attending the 2005 Northwest Division Conference of MENC: The National Association for Music Education.

[Your name], who [describe your teaching experience or level or include other pertinent information], attended the meeting to [describe your goals and reasons].

[Your last name] was one of thousands of music educators who convened in Bellevue, Washington, February 18–20, 2005, to experience workshops, exhibits, and performances by school ensembles and by the All-Northwest Honor Groups, consisting of more than 900 of the most musically accomplished high school students in the Northwest region of the United States. Other highlights included an Evening of Jazz, music education exhibits, and a Get America Singing . . . Again! program by Kirby Shaw.

"[A quote describing your experience at the conference, how it will help you in your teaching, and the importance of music in school is appropriate to add here]," says [your name].

Figure 3.2   Press release template (from MENC)

Becoming a public relations expert gives your students the chance to shine—and get recognized for it. Everyone who comes into contact with your program is a potential instrumental music supporter, and the more of them, the better. Show them what you do and how well you do it, and just watch the ruckus they make if your program is endangered!

Four

Time and Student Management

Current school policies place ever-increasing time constraints on most ensemble directors, meaning that efficiency in rehearsal, though certainly a priority in the past, is even more critical now. To combat limited rehearsal time, I have modified some time-tested practices that flow from basic teaching and learning principles. I review some general rehearsal planning and procedures tenets and provide some specific techniques that you can adapt to fit any rehearsal environment. They have a successful track record in rural, suburban, and urban schools.

The key elements to success with limited rehearsal time are action and adaptation. Action through involvement with advocacy efforts in local, state, and national campaigns facilitates public awareness of diminished rehearsal time and other cuts to instrumental music programs. Adapting rehearsal preparation and practices helps to battle time constraints after cuts have occurred. Effective rehearsal planning and procedures are imperative for the many directors who, like me, consistently race the clock while trying to cultivate excellent programs.

In spite of concentrated advocacy and publicity efforts, like many directors, I have faced near-crippling cuts in rehearsal time in some of my previous programs, though in retrospect the cuts would have probably been much worse without my publicity efforts. Faced with these inevitable reductions, I continued my advocacy and publicity efforts, but decided to also combat the problem internally by evaluating my occasionally inefficient teaching practice and program infrastructure.

Effective student management and discipline are critical components of efficient rehearsals. Student management consists of proactive measures teachers take to ensure the environment is conducive to learning; for example, room set-up and lesson preparation. Student discipline is ensuring a learning environment by addressing undesired behavior. The two can be contrasted easily this way: student management is proactive, while student discipline is reactive. Student discipline is the most significant challenge for new teachers, particularly when working with underserved students. Malleable enough to fit any teaching and learning environment, the following practices stem from sound principles first introduced in undergraduate education classes and apply to practical, real-world situations.

LESSON PLANNING

Planning rehearsals that account for every minute available maximizes teaching time and curbs behavior problems. Though seemingly obvious, knowledge of the score and other musical material planned for the rehearsal saves time. There are no quick routes to score study and lesson planning; they simply take time outside rehearsal.

Battisti and Garofalo (1990) warn that "[t]o communicate the expressive potential of a musical composition to an ensemble in an effective and efficient manner, a conductor must first acquire an understanding of the score" (p. 1). Thorough score analysis that encompasses both musical and technical elements allows directors to understand the music and develop ways to meaningfully and efficiently share it with students.

Even after several years of teaching certain pieces, I still study scores for both musical and technical details that might pose performance problems and then carefully write lesson plans. "An outstanding rehearsal is well organized and planned in advance" (Blocher & Miles, 1999, p. 37). Like most experienced teachers, my lesson plans appear confusing to others because I use an abbreviation system that I have developed to save time, but they still include effective lesson plan components. One crucial item in the lesson plan that I still diligently include is the "reflection" or "evaluation" portion at the end of the plan. After rehearsal, I note what worked, what did not, problem areas in the score, and any other details needed to plan the next lesson. The few minutes it takes to reflect in writing saves me time in the next rehearsal because I know exactly what we need to accomplish.

PHYSICAL SET-UP AND ROUTINE

Another fundamental management element that contributes to efficiency in any classroom involves the set-up of the physical environment before instruction—also known as "controlling the environment before it controls you." Make sure you set up the room so you can move about as freely as possible during rehearsal. Doing so allows you to move closer to students who might misbehave. Directors who "mix it up" and move about the room are simply more interesting to students. Mobility free of obstruction enables directors to have access to students who may need individual assistance or to monitor and coach peer tutors or teacher's aides assisting new students or exceptional learners.

Directors also hear and see ensembles differently from different areas of the room. Critically looking and listening nearer to instrument sections located farther away from the podium assists in identifying problems with technique as well as helping with aural error detection.

Students can help prepare for rehearsal by distributing music and putting equipment in place. Be sure to put the daily repertory order on the board, and place lesson plans, written reminders, announcements, blank paper, and a pencil on the conductor's stand for "Notes to Self" during rehearsal.

I also make sure I have baton, tuner, metronome, and other instructional aids in place near the podium. Any trip out of the room not only wastes instruction time but also compromises orderliness as students begin off-task behaviors. To further alleviate misbehavior when students enter the room, I always try to stand at the podium or near the front door to greet them. I discourage any horseplay and help students mentally prepare for the rehearsal by playing music recordings that relate to the repertory planned for the day.

Students should know rehearsal routines such as instrument storage and tuning procedures. For example, even when students are seated and setting up instruments, I do not allow any playing because we warm up together after class begins. Some directors—particularly those of older students—train students to warm up and even tune independently, but I find that silent preparation creates a more orderly environment for younger students. Such order prevents unnecessary distraction and helps keep students focused on the work ahead.

Whatever routines or procedures you institute, it is critical that they are followed consistently and that students understand precisely what it is you expect them to do. Rather than simple verbal instructions, you will also need to physically rehearse procedures with students (Wong & Wong, 2005). Grinder (1993) states that visual directions "increase the clarity of the message and double the length of the memory" (p. 30). Thus, for multi-step procedures such as entering the classroom and preparing instruments for rehearsal, you should post procedure in clear, concise words. Also consider adding icons for very young students, English language learners, and students with exceptional needs.

Canter (2006) recommends a technique called behavioral narration to help reinforce expectations while rehearsing procedures. First, clearly describe the procedure, preferably represented in written form and icons if there are more than one or two steps. As students physically move through each step (e. g., enter classroom quietly, assemble instruments, etc.), identify students who are following directions without overt praise. For example,

"Carlos and Alyssa are entering the room quietly" or "Leslie is assembling her clarinet near the floor so the clarinet does not break if dropped." These behavioral narrations serve to remind all students of each step and the precise way to perform it.

Though counter to many behavior management systems, Canter (2006), Kohn (1999), and others recommend avoiding praise to motivate students in order to better instill intrinsic motivation generated from students themselves for completing tasks properly rather than creating reliance on extrinsic rewards from the teacher. This is difficult to realize as many district- or school-wide management systems hinge on praise and other rewards. However, I have found that many students, particularly in middle school and above, do not like being singled out, even when exhibiting positive behaviors. When providing behavior narration for students, a judgment statement such as "*I like how* Queshawn is sitting quietly" can be simply phrased, "Queshawn is sitting quietly." Similarly, refrain from phrases such as "good job," "nice work," and so on, as these are examples of teacher approval that can curb students' self-satisfaction in completing tasks and may humiliate them in front of peers.

AVOIDING EXCESS TALKING

You can easily observe restless body language in rehearsals run by directors who talk too much. For new concepts, I use the learning style sequence discussed in the next chapter, which requires auditory, visual, and tactile or kinesthetic representations of material. For verbal corrections, directors save time and maximize student attentiveness by making very brief, specific comments that include both a succinct statement of the problem and a means to rectify it. Directors maintain rehearsal focus if they remember to "teach more; talk less" (Moore, Batey, and Royse 2002, p. 31).

To further expedite my direction with less talk, I have devised hand signs for common problems such as intonation, hand position, and embouchure that I use while conducting that, together with eye contact, quickly make individual players aware of a problem without the embarrassment of public scrutiny. Of course, the success of these nonverbal cues depends on the ability of students to watch my conducting. The time I spend training students to respond to conducting gestures and other cues alleviates the need for excess verbiage.

REPAIRS

Save time by avoiding instrument repairs during rehearsal. Of course, students should maintain their own instruments, but the extent to which this is possible depends upon the age of the student. Directors should teach and reinforce proper care of instruments and monitor student efforts in lessons so that stuck valves and other maintenance-related mishaps occur less often in rehearsal.

Most directors keep extra reeds and oils on hand for emergency use, but I also have at least one loaner instrument available for every instrument type—two for clarinets and flutes. If the school does not own them, instrument dealers may lend them for the school year. A necessary accessory to loaner instruments is plenty of disinfectant to sterilize mouthpieces. When budgets are tight, inexpensive, mint-flavored rubbing alcohol (available at most pharmacies) transferred to a spray bottle is a quick sterilizer, but to avoid possible mouthpiece discoloration, you can use antibacterial dish or hand soap and water.

Note that students play better on their own instruments, to which they are accustomed. Any more than a couple of forgotten instrument episodes requires some attention by the director, which often includes a phone call home. As directors work with students and parents to remember instruments, and when instruments are out for repair, loaners help keep students progressing.

STUDENT MANAGEMENT AND DISCIPLINE

Student management and discipline (also known as classroom management) is vital to effective rehearsals and a particularly challenging issue for directors. Participation in instrumental music is almost always voluntary, and a director who is too permissive loses effectiveness and time in rehearsals, while a director who is too stern loses students. Remember, a carefully planned rehearsal keeps students focused and alleviates most behavior problems.

Directors can keep behavior problems from slowing down rehearsal with a policy that consists of fair, consistently enforced, and clearly defined rules with consequences—basic principles covered in most classroom management classes. Because I am fair and consistent, my students often describe me in their vernacular as "strict" (enforcing appropriate behavior), but not "mean" (uncaring, hostile). Students actually prefer "strict" directors, but few will participate in the programs of "mean" ones. Though designed for elementary and middle school students, the following classroom management techniques also work for high school students if rewards and consequences are modified.

One central principle to managing students effectively through consistent procedures and policies is composure (Bailey, 2001). This is particularly important with respect to discipline, which often means assigning consequences for inappropriate behavior. Once a teacher is angered, management efforts are thwarted as he or she loses control of the situation and teaches students what *not* to do. Bailey (2001) describes composure as "being the person you want others to become" (p. 25). She further points out that "no one can make you angry without your permission" and that it is important that we "remain calm enough to teach children how to behave by example" (p. 25). Further, if we want students to learn social competence, such as being polite, we must demonstrate this. The same is true for proper dress and any other behavior integral to success in school and work. With underserved students, hostility by the teacher will almost always be matched by hostility by students, particularly in middle and high school. Remaining in control by remaining calm is probably one of the most important principles in student management, but the least realized in real-world classrooms.

Individual Behavior

Mendler, Curwin, and Mendler (2008) advise to be consistent, but flexible and "to be fair, not necessarily equal" (p. 86). Some students with exceptional needs may have behavior needs and formalized plans that require flexibility. Some students will sit quietly for the entire class, and others will need multiple interventions. A rigid system will not manage all of these students effectively. A plan that accounts for individual and group behavior is effective as it provides flexibility and adequately accounts for the varied types of behavior issues.

At the onset of behavior problems, I use a couple of techniques usually covered in classroom management classes: eye contact and temporarily moving within closer proximity to the off-task student(s). Mendler, Curwin, and Mendler (2008) incorporate these in the "PEP technique" (p. 105). *PEP* is the acronym for *privacy, eye contact,* and *proximity,* and it is best used during the early stages of student misbehavior. For example, if a student is disrupting class, approach him or her during the natural course of the lesson, quickly get down to his or her level (*proximity*), make strong *eye contact,* and tell him or her as quietly (*privacy*), politely (modeling the behaviors we wish in our students), but firmly as possible, "Please stop." Shortly after, another student is exhibiting desired behavior. Using the same PEP technique, say to the student, "Your grip on the stick is much more relaxed since rehearsal yesterday and the drum is more resonant because of it. Thank you." In both cases, it is critical that the teacher immediately move away from the student to avoid any further discussion. This is critical for the technique to work. If the student tries to engage the teacher further, the teacher should not respond. Further, this technique is only effective if you provide feedback for both negative and positive behaviors. The rest of the class will not know which kind of feedback you are providing to individuals, which decreases chances students will feel humiliated when you employ the technique.

If verbal reminders do not suffice, I move to a two-card system that everyone understands but that minimizes public humiliation. I place an index card with the word "Reminder" written in blue ink on the music stand behind the music folder of the student. Although other students are aware of the reprimand, it is less severe than a verbal admonishment and requires no discussion. It merely warns students that they need to monitor their behavior. If the student fails to follow rehearsal rules after receiving the warning card, I place a "Report to Parent" card, written in red ink, behind the folder. This "report" can constitute either a phone call or a note mailed home that identifies some positive attributes of the students, a description of the incident, and a way to address it. The card can also be a "lunch detention" or other consequence established by you or employed school-wide. As with the PEP technique, you can also distribute cards that identify positive behavior as well.

I usually do not have to issue more than two red cards at the beginning of the year, as word gets out about my parental phone call, letter, or home visit. Students learn that I commit to keeping order in rehearsal. Whether blue or red, after rehearsal students must return the cards to me, at which point we privately discuss behavior and expectations. I include positive comments along with a clear statement of the problem and solution, just as I do when I talk to their parents.

Community-Building and Group Behavior

Classrooms are microcosms of the greater society and so are an opportune environment to teach positive social behaviors. A harmonious classroom environment is inclusive of all students, regardless of individual differences. Vanston (1992), Kluth (2003), and Udvari-Solner and Kluth (2008) offer many community-building and learning strategies that foster accepting attitudes. As students are tracked less and exceptional learners included in general education, wide variance in students is becoming the norm, yet we must educate them together in harmonious and productive ensembles. For this reason, instituting community-building activities throughout the school year is effective in fostering esprit de corps as well as minimizing insults and bullying among students.

Here is one example of community building I find particularly effective. My ensembles begin the year by forming a circle—or multiple circles in larger ensembles—and making a "unity web" with a ball of yarn. The first student holds the end of the yarn ball in one hand, states his or her name, and tosses the ball of yarn across the circle to a second peer. The second peer forms a line with the yarn by grasping the yarn piece with one hand. He or she repeats the name of the first student and tosses the ball of yarn to a third student, who then has to repeat the name of the first and second student. This continues until a web of yarn is created among students. The activity serves to teach names of members in the ensemble, but I also explain that the yarn connects us all together and that it is this unity that will help us become a great ensemble. After a couple of months, we'll repeat this activity, but instead of names, the first student pays the second student a compliment, then tosses the yarn ball. The second student pays a third student across the circle a compliment and tosses the yarn ball, and so on. Compliments cannot be about physical characteristics (e.g., hair, clothing), and must focus on character traits (e. g., willingness to share) or musician-like traits (e.g., accurate intonation). This is new for most students and will take some encouragement, but the effect is powerful in building cohesive and inclusive communities in ensembles.

Because misbehavior often involves more than two or three students and peer pressure or support is powerful, I have instituted a group goal that students earn together during rehearsal. I used to have a system where students would "lose their marbles" for behavior infractions. If all marbles were lost, there would be something desired taken away. However, I found that individual students were often blamed when group rewards were not earned.

Now I use a system that is not punitive and builds community. Serving as a team-building technique, students must earn, rather than lose, a prescribed number of marbles. This way, rewards are individualized, as a particularly challenging student can earn a reward for the group by not exhibiting outbursts for several minutes, while another student may earn a marble for assisting an English language learner or exceptional student during rehearsal. Both are viewed equally in the eyes of peers, as they have earned the same thing towards the desired activity. Students with challenging behaviors are more valued and serve to gain, rather than lose, rewards, which is typical in many management systems.

If the group can gain a certain number of marbles (or checkmarks, etc.), they earn Preferred Activity Time, or P.A.T. (Jones, 2000). This P.A.T. is often a game that ties directly to lesson goals. For example, they may earn reading rhythms by playing a rhythm reading game at the end of rehearsal that is structured after organized sports ("rhythm football," "rhythm volleyball"; see also the game in Chapter 2). The key to effective P.A.T. is finding activities that students want and that reinforce music skills targeted in the lesson. I have found that these games are appropriate for all ages, as students never lose their sense of fun, though games will have to be tailored for specific age levels, of course.

Some directors claim that they expect and receive complete silence during the entire rehearsal. This is unreasonable to expect with younger students during rehearsals that last more than 30 minutes. Attention problems occur after extended periods of the same activity, even a naturally engaging one like playing an instrument. If activities are prolonged, students become increasingly less attentive toward the end of rehearsal, and I lose time trying to engage them. Varying activities throughout the rehearsal keeps them focused. During particularly intense rehearsals, I provide a break by leading the group in a quick movement activity involving concepts covered in rehearsal (rhythm patterns, dynamics, and so on). These movements help relax tense playing muscles and release the excess energy that might lead to behavior issues that interrupt rehearsal.

Though not recommended by some directors, I tell students they have 30 seconds to a minute between rehearsal segments to get out the next piece. I usually allow controlled individual conversations pertinent to the activities at hand during this time to provide a brief period of respite between the intense periods of concentration needed to play. Students often use this time to help each other solve performance problems. I encourage and reward this whenever possible, particularly because I have revolving enrollment and often assign tutors to students who have begun later in the year.

Even during brief periods of transition you must maintain an orderly climate or you waste time trying to regain rehearsal focus. When groups of people are called to order, immediate cessation of talking rarely occurs, and the leader usually repeats the call a few times as students conclude their thoughts before ending conversations. Rather than asking for silence several times, I make the request for quiet once and then count down by five from about 15 seconds (15, 10, 5, 0), which controls the flow of rehearsal while allowing students a chance to prepare percussion instruments and otherwise transition to the next piece. In order to be effective, you must clearly discuss procedures and routines and practice them with students. Remain consistent with your expectations.

Students as Helpers and Leaders

I expect students to help me with rehearsal efficiency. With my beginners, I notice that they have varying levels of independence. Consequently, I used to waste rehearsal time by providing solutions that students themselves could easily remedy. Now, at the beginning of the year, I demonstrate how students can avoid excessive teacher direction particularly when preparing for rehearsal.

For example, if students come to me about not having a music stand, I indicate the extras in the corner of the room and explain that they are expected to quietly get one. If a student raises his or her hand to report that another student won't move over to provide enough room for a large instrument, I clearly articulate my expectation that all students work together to provide ample space and that I am available to help with irresolvable conflicts, but I expect ensemble members to work as a team in rehearsal. Of course, I must intervene at times, but a consistent expectation that students rely on their own resourcefulness—both as individuals and as team players—frees rehearsals from unnecessary, time-consuming mediation.

To further aid student independence, I designate one to three leaders in each instrument group. Though often veterans or students with leadership qualities at first, to help community-building, you should institute a rotating policy where all students have opportunity to lead. Section leaders answer questions from less experienced students, pass out notices, check sections at the end of rehearsals to ensure that all equipment and music is put away correctly, or deal with frequent problems, such as lost music or missing percussion equipment. Clearly define their power from the beginning, and deal with any abuses immediately. I seldom have problems with student leaders and they greatly expedite time-consuming tasks.

While lack of rehearsal time is irritating if not downright overwhelming, don't let it get the best of you. Plan your time well and let your students become your allies in generating productive rehearsals. You might not be able to control the amount of time you have, but you can control what you do.

Students Who Do Not Seem to Care

In spite of our best efforts with management and discipline, there are students who are still particularly challenging. These students often do not have parents to whom you can go for support. In these cases, the best solution is to try to establish a personal connection with those students. "Personal connection means finding ways to create an atmosphere of trust, so that students want to learn what we have to share" (Mendler, 2001, p. 21).

There are several ways to establish positive relationships with students, and the sources cited in this chapter contain several. In general, to build positive, trusting relationships that foster respect, we should try to recognize each student in a positive way each day (Canter, 2006, p. 211). One way I have found success with students who are particularly hard to reach is through the "2 x 10" technique (Mendler, 2001). Make a commitment to relationship build for 2 minutes each day for 10 consecutive days, or as close to this time frame as your schedule allows. "During those two minutes, you cannot do or say anything related to correcting the student's behavior or telling the student what he must do differently to be successful in class. . . . By the 10th day, teachers report improved communication with the student, as well as evidence of better behavior" (Mendler, 2001, p. 25).

If you are really taxed for time outside of class, Fay and Funk (1995) recommend the "one-minute intervention" (p. 21), which takes less time and might be implemented during class. Approach the student six times over the next three school weeks with a statement that begins "I noticed . . . ," completing the statement with something honest and true. As with the 2 x 10 technique, do not focus on classroom behavior, but something more personal. This might be done in conjunction with the PEP technique detailed above.

Positive relationships between teacher and students must be established before learning can begin (Comer, 2004). It is more difficult to do this in some schools than others, particularly those with underserved students. Yet establishing these relationships is the critical first step in effective student management and discipline, and your consistent endeavors in this area will pay large dividends in creating ensembles with students who want to learn and perform well.

Five

Multisensory Teaching

There has been recent scrutiny about the relevance or even existence of discrete learning styles (Coffield, Moseley, Hall, & Ecclestone, 2004; Pashler, McDaniel, Rohrer, & Bjork, 2008). This research has concluded that several experimental designs are flawed and there is "conceptual confusion" (Coffield, Moseley, Hall, & Ecclestone, 2004, p. 135) with contradictions amongst the various theories. Actually, learning style researchers themselves have long extolled the need for a unified concept and terminology for learning style theory to be useful (Dunn, DeBello, Brennan, Krimsky, & Murrain, 1981).

Even though there is considerable debate, the concept is important to educators because many learning style theories center on sensory inputs; that is, sight, sound, smell, taste, and touch. Even if learning style preference theories are refuted, many educators recommend a multisensory approach to teaching. Baines (2008) explains:

> Two of the greatest challenges for teachers in the years ahead will be student engagement and achievement. Multisensory learning techniques provide an effective, highly adaptable method for addressing both. . . . When students invoke more than one sense, they tend to interact with the material more intensely and thereby retain what they have learned for longer periods of time. (p. x)

With respect to students with exceptional needs, Baines writes that "the research base that affirms the power of multisensory approaches with learning-disabled children and adults is vast and growing" (p. xi). Multisensory approaches are also standard pedagogy for English language learners. Researchers have also suggested learning style preferences according to gender (Sax, 2005) and even gender and ethnicity/race (Kunjufu, 1990, 2005). With respect to all learners in general, multisensory learning is more engaging and yields higher retention (Baines, 2008). Thus, approaching your teaching by accessing multiple sensory inputs is important whether from a learning style theory or a multisensory learning perspective.

I believe that there is convincing support for both learning style and multisensory learning approaches. In fact, it is the single most effective teaching approach I use because my ensembles consist of large numbers of students with exceptional needs and English language learners. It is important to note that English language learners and students with exceptional needs are two distinct populations but often require the same attention to teaching strategies that focus on auditory, visual, and tactile-kinesthetic abilities to process information.

Like their students, directors respond to certain learning styles or sensory inputs better than others, and it can be challenging for directors to collect and incorporate teaching techniques for all ways of learning. The following teaching sequence accommodates all learning styles and most stimuli processing modes and becomes second nature with a little initial planning and practice. The benefits outweigh the effort, as directors who account for both individual and cultural learning styles reach and teach more students.

Teachers often use the lecture-style method of instruction, and its ineffectiveness for nonauditory learners is well known. I vividly remember observing students who seemed to not listen to my explanations. Actually, they were quite attentive; they were simply looking at pictures or diagrams in the book that showed the concept that I was verbally describing. The "light went on" for some students because the visual representations in the method book taught them more effectively than my lecture.

Like many teachers, I made largely verbal presentations, and further study convinced me that I could have taught more effectively and saved time if I had accounted for different learning styles. I now use a teaching sequence in rehearsal and lessons that maximizes my teaching effectiveness by accommodating the different types of learners in my ensembles. Recently, I have also considered strategies that account for learning styles that have a cultural foundation.

First, we must understand these learning styles. Several models describe individual styles, but I have found that planning instruction by adding Fleming's (1995) read/write learning style to Celli-Sarasin's (1999) auditory, visual, and kinesthetic model easily and adequately accommodates diverse learning styles. Understanding the characteristics of four learning styles prepares you to plan effective instruction.

DIFFERENT TYPES OF LEARNERS

Read/write learners "reveal a preference for accessing information from printed words" (Fleming, 1995, p. 2), which is the most common method of information exchange in educational settings. These students learn by seeing and writing printed words and are prolific note-takers in lecture-style presentations. Though they are usually successful in lecture-style presentations, their preferred learning style needs consideration in instrumental music settings.

Auditory learners, as the term suggests, approach education experiences effectively through listening. These learners process verbal instruction easily. It seems that all students drawn to music would be auditory learners because of its aural nature, but an assessment of learning styles in rehearsal reveals that this is not the case. As Gardner (1999) posits, a student with high musical intelligence can have a preference for any one of the four modes of processing. Therefore, lecture-style demonstrations, group discussions, and modeling with the voice or instrument may help only some of your music students process information effectively. This may be the only effective input for some students with exceptional needs.

Visual learners often have trouble in rehearsal because directors usually use verbal instruction. These students benefit from graphic representations and visual demonstrations of skills and concepts. A teacher's aural example may not be enough for visual learners; actually seeing a diagram or "picture" of the sound may help. This is especially true for English language learners and many students with exceptional needs as they can see pictures and icons for words they do not understand.

Kinesthetic learners learn by doing. This type of learner has been traditionally the most neglected in education settings (Celli-Sarasin, 1999). Fortunately, instrumental music easily caters to this learning style because of the hands-on nature of playing an instrument. But the built-in interaction with the instrument does not always help this type of learner understand new skills, concepts, or content. These learners often benefit from teaching techniques that allow them to "feel" the concept or skill away from the instrument first. Kinesthetic activities are often especially helpful for students diagnosed with attention deficit disorder/attention deficit hyperactivity disorder, commonly known as ADD/ADHD (Armstrong, 1999).

When introducing new information, I use a teaching sequence that accounts for all four types of learners. Although each step addresses a different learning style, all students benefit from each step because it helps learners process information through modes that differ from those that they use naturally. Celli-Sarasin (1999) elaborates:

[I]t is not necessary to limit tactile learners to the tactile, visual learners to the visual, and auditory learners to the auditory. Students naturally gravitate to parts of the lesson with which they feel most comfortable. However, if lessons are designed holistically . . . all students will experience all parts of the lesson and have the chance to learn through their areas of strength, as well as develop their weaker style areas. (p. 85)

The combination of a holistic teaching model and a practical teaching sequence makes my rehearsals effective.

The first step ("hear it") includes demonstrations of the desired behavior and sound and helps auditory learners. This step may also include verbal review of prior knowledge and group discussions, which activate the interest of all students. In the second step ("see it"), present a graphic representation and accommodate read/write learners by writing words that explain the graphics. The third step ("feel it") appeals to tactile or kinesthetic learners because it provides a way to understand through the body. All students understand and demonstrate the new skill or concept before becoming encumbered with the instrument, which is especially important for beginning students whose executive playing skills are not yet second nature. Once students show they understand a skill by simulating it away from the instrument, they then demonstrate it while playing.

TEACHING SEQUENCE TO ACCOMMODATE DIFFERENT LEARNING STYLES

Concept: Proper Articulation for Winds

Let students:

1. Hear what it sounds like. Engage auditory learners through verbal analogies or class discussion. Make sure to demonstrate the skill or concept with your voice or instrument if applicable. For example, explain to beginning students that the proper articulation and note length should sound like the notes are almost touching, with the tongue separating each note.
2. See what it sounds like. Draw a diagram or model. Be sure to include word descriptions for read/write learners. Figure 5.1 shows a visual example of proper articulation and note length for beginners.
3. Feel what it sounds like away from the instrument with the body. Students can demonstrate the example by "air playing," where they finger the desired note on the instrument, but tongue quarter notes while forming the embouchure away from the mouthpiece. Brass players can do the same, but buzz on the mouthpiece.

4. Do it on the instrument. Monitor progress and repeat steps above if necessary.

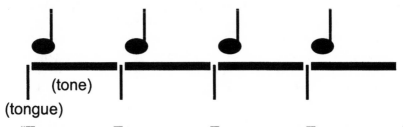

(tone)

(tongue)

"TaaaaaaaaaTaaaaaaaaaaTaaaaaaaaaaTaaaaaaaaaa"

Figure 5.1   Visual example of proper articulation and note length for beginners

Concept: Tuning for Strings and Winds

Let students:

1. Hear what it sounds like. Explain that a pleasing sound on string or wind instruments does not occur by simply pressing strings, keys, or valves. Demonstrate "out-of-tune-ness" by playing in tune first. Then play sharp and flat. Play a unison pitch with a student and bend the pitch sharp and flat relative to the student's pitch. Guide students' perception of the "wobbles" (beats) that occur when you play sharp or flat. Conclude by playing in tune with the student.
2. See what it sounds like. Play a pitch in tune as indicated by an electronic tuner. Then play pitches out of tune while having students note the sharpness and flatness indicated by the electronic tuner. Draw a picture such as the one in Figure 5.2 to further aid the beginner. (I continue to use this graphic as a visual reminder to students even after they have a basic grasp of the basic concept of "in-tune-ness.")
3. Feel what it sounds like away from the instrument. Have students sing pitches "in the bull's eye" (in tune) as indicated by an electronic

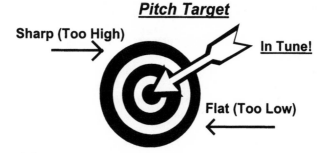

Figure 5.2   Pitch target

tuner. Next, they sing intentionally sharp and flat. They conclude by singing pitches in the bull's eye (in tune).

4. Do it on the instrument. Two students play a unison pitch on similar instruments and try to get rid of the "wobbles" (beats) in the air by having one student adjust the embouchure and the length of the instrument. Also have individual students play pitches using the tuner. After they accurately play a pitch in tune, have them try to bend the pitch sharp and flat according to the tuner. Conclude by playing pitches in tune.

If you observe that students need more help to demonstrate understanding, move through the sequence again, but try a different explanation. Use a graphic representation, followed by a new demonstration away from the instrument. I have found that a review of the visual aid ("see it") and the movement away from the instrument ("feel it") usually suffices.

You can learn new teaching techniques through method books, professional journals, or by attending clinics at professional conferences. In time, a teaching sequence such as this one becomes seamless. My experience has shown that it saves time because teaching becomes more differentiated and diverse learners grasp skills and concepts more quickly.

Though typical learners have a preferred way of processing (a detailed discussion of exceptional learners follows in the next chapter), they can still process information to some extent in the other three modes. Many so-called at-risk learners, or those with a perceived high likelihood of failure in school, benefit from the sequence because their avoidance behaviors often stem from learning disabilities.

CULTURAL LEARNING STYLES

How cultural values become manifested in specific culture-based learning styles is a current hot topic. Colarusso and O'Rourke (2004) describe the conflicting ways in which teachers approach students:

> One culture might encourage spontaneity and creativity in children, and yet another teach the importance of restraint in all behaviors. . . . One teacher might perceive a student's shouting out of answers and ideas as disruptive, while another teacher sees it as a reflection of the student's interest and active participation in the learning process. Individuals from different cultures often view the world from vastly different perspectives. (p. 19)

Varying cultural learning styles affect how directors plan and deliver instruction.

Lessons that relate to students' lives and involve social interaction are recommended for many African American (Hale, 2001; Kunjufu, 1986, 1990, 2002; Ladson-Billings, 1994) and Hispanic students (Kuykendall, 1992). As a tenet of constructivist pedagogy, lessons relevant to personal experience benefit all learners (Boardman, 2002; Brooks & Brooks, 1993). The more "people-oriented" (Kunjufu, 1990, p. 13) learning style attributed to some cultures has also been observed generally in adolescent students, when peers replace the significance of adults (Steinberg, 1996). Most instrumental music students in the midst of adolescence are "field-dependent learners" (Kuykendall, 1992, Chap. 3), motivated by social and personal relevance.

Directors can structure some activities to involve working with peers. For example, practice buddies involve older students, usually a sibling, extended relative, family friend, or neighbor, who checks on younger instrumental music students at home between lessons. I have had accomplished eighth-grade students choose a fourth- or fifth-grade buddy to help with home practice during the younger student's first year of study. After I prepare them for how best to help, the eighth graders practice with the younger students once a week after school.

This form of interaction proves particularly beneficial, as all students are motivated to some degree by their social context. This is also a way to build community within ensembles and amongst ensembles in your program. Further, multiple older students deepen their own understanding as tutors (a benefit of cooperative learning), and younger students are encouraged to practice by a significant peer. Younger students also look forward to being practice buddies when they reach eighth grade.

Directors sensitive to the social dynamics of student relationships prove more effective in reaching and teaching their students. Fortunately, the ensembles naturally create a socially relevant context. An ensemble requires the cultivation of esprit de corps, or the "one-for-all-ness" in the ensemble, as opposed to the accomplishments of individuals. I often tell students that audience members are not usually trained musicians that can pinpoint strengths and weaknesses of individual players. Typical listeners generally describe the performance as either good or bad and give praise or criticism to the entire group. Students must support one another so that the entire group is rewarded for collaborative successes. Such teamwork frames a positive social learning environment and provides meaning for field-dependent learners.

Social dynamics can make getting singled out of a group for scrutiny a particularly uncomfortable experience. Like issues associated with social and personal relevance, heightened sensitivity could stem from cultural values or simply from the developmental age of the student. Instead of addressing single players, directors should address the entire section, or simply refer to groups of players: "How could that have been better? Do you hear some instruments not blending? We all must be listening and adjusting so that our sounds blend together." Directors should describe (or have students describe) the problem and recommend or solicit solutions from students in ways that minimize public humiliation and competition among players and to emphasize the importance of every player within the group.

Students learn according to the ways in which they process information within their social and cultural contexts. Adapting instruction to accommodate varied styles of learning engenders thorough and streamlined instruction.

Six

Including Exceptional Learners

Although many directors approach inclusion with apprehension, reservations usually prove unfounded so long as directors adequately prepare themselves to instruct students with exceptional needs. Preparation includes professional study by the director and collaboration with special education and clinical staff, administrators, parents, and the students themselves. A plan that realistically accounts for student strengths and limitations helps directors and students get started. Diligent assessment in light of goals for all students fosters a successful, inclusive classroom.

The Education for All Handicapped Children Act (1975), now Individuals with Disabilities Education Act (IDEA), has led to mainstreaming and inclusion of exceptional learners in all school program areas, to the extent possible in the "least restrictive environment" (P. L. No. 94-142). Though special education is broad and includes gifted students, the term *exceptional learner* or *student with exceptional needs* in the present discussion refers to students with learning disabilities, cognitive deficits, and physical.

It is wrong to assume that inclusion is a choice. In fact, it is the law. The most current IDEA revision requires even more accountability for schools and teachers for inclusive practices (Adamek & Darrow, 2005). Further, Section 504 of the Rehabilitation Act of 1973 offers protection from discrimination because of disability. Yet exceptional learners are seldom included in instrumental music ensembles. All students have a right to participate in all school activities to the extent they are capable, and it is your responsibility to include and even recruit students with exceptional needs as you would typical students.

Inclusion causes concern for many directors because they feel that accommodating students with special needs will lead to rehearsal disruption and diminished performance quality. The "least restrictive environment" refers to the satisfactory learning progress of typical students as well as that of exceptional students. Therefore, directors need to balance an individual learner's special needs with the needs of the other ensemble members. To do this, directors usually require support from special education staff, administration, and parents. A collaborative effort ensures enriching experiences for all ensemble participants.

Despite any disability, it may be quite possible that exceptional learners simply won't dedicate the necessary level of commitment to home practice and other program expectations. Regardless of special need, student commitment should predicate participation and resultant success, and students and parents must understand this from the beginning. In my experience, lack of commitment, as with typical learners, is the most frequent reason exceptional learners do not succeed in instrumental music.

Of course, if dedicated exceptional learners exhibit performance or behavior issues directly attributable to special needs, directors may need to provide further modification. Directors might consider recruiting, consultation with staff and parents, selecting appropriate instruments, preparing and involving student peers, and music modification when including exceptional learners.

RECRUITING

Directors often recruit exceptional learners in the same sessions in which they recruit typical students. If scheduling these sessions during the school day, directors should check with classroom teachers to see if students need added assistance to participate. If this is the case, teachers or teachers' assistants familiar with these special needs should accompany students.

In particular, the skills assessment portion of the session, if included, may require adaptation for some students. Classroom staff can provide extra assistance to individuals while the director administers the assessment for typical students. In some cases, administering assessments at a different time ensures that you can accurately determine the skills of exceptional students. For example, if a student has difficulty understanding responses provided on the answer sheet, he or she will likely provide incorrect answers, but they have nothing to do with music skills. Students may need more detailed instructions and practice questions or to respond orally rather than with written responses. Special education teachers familiar with particular students can guide modifications.

Some exceptional students may not have the cognitive skills to indicate a preference about whether or not to participate in instrumental music study. Recruiting drives may miss other students who do not participate in general classrooms frequently, but such students usually take part in either mainstreamed or specialized music classes. General music teachers can recommend students who show interest in playing classroom instruments, and special education staff can provide further insight as to the appropriateness of instrumental music study for their students.

WORKING WITH COLLEAGUES AND PARENTS

IDEA specifies that students with disabilities ages three through twenty-one have a right to individualized instruction detailed in the Individualized Education Plan (IEP). Students with disabilities that do not require the level of services in an IEP may still have accommodations or adaptations stipulated in a 504 Plan, which is "derived from Section 504 of the 1973 Health and Rehabilitation Act" (Hammel & Hourigan, 2011, p. 67). It is important to note that all teachers working with students who have disabilities must adhere to IEPs and 504 plans and so must be familiar with them. Most instrumental music teachers do not have special education backgrounds, so the documents might be confusing for them. Many schools have simplified summaries for non–special education staff to review. However, I have found it most helpful to go through IEPs and 504 plans with special education staff to avoid confusion and ensure a consistent education program for students.

Approach decisions about instrumental study as a team. Special education staff should make recommendations based on expertise as well as experience with particular students. When considering the best way to include an exceptional learner, I confer first with special education teachers and, if warranted, psychologists and physical and occupational therapists. I want to have adequate information when recommending instruments and possible adaptations before I make decisions concerning exceptional students and their parents.

After this consultation, I am better equipped to discuss inclusion options with parents. Some parents have had to fight to have their children included in other school programs and quickly develop an aggressive position if they sense unreceptive directors. Instead, use a proactive approach that respects parental input, and you will garner their support. My experience shows that parents support teachers who genuinely commit to including exceptional learners. A realistic plan that respects the needs of individual learners while accounting for the interests of all other students in the ensemble usually proves possible.

Sometimes parents may resist the recommendations made by special education staff and director. They may not think that their child should have individual lessons instead of group lessons, or ensemble participation with the support of a teacher's aide. The parent might feel that their child "loves music" and won't exhibit the same inappropriate behavior in instrumental music classes that warrants extra support in a general education classroom. I never assume I know students better than parents, but I insist that students receive the same support in the instrumental music class as their other classes until I get to know the student. I always encourage parents to attend the first lesson or two so that we can monitor progress together. They provide helpful input and their presence supports my efforts. Special education staff can observe and provide additional input.

Directors usually need to take the initiative to learn about the nature of specific disabilities. An increasing amount of information has become available regarding several disabilities and how to address them when playing musical instruments, particularly in publications such as MENC's *Music Educators Journal* and *Teaching Music*. Adamek and Darrow (2005) have also compiled a good deal of current information for music teachers in *Music in Special Education*.

Lack of support from school personnel can lead to unsuccessful inclusion. For example, teachers' aides often support exceptional students, but their breaks are sometimes scheduled during general music classes and other "specials." Lack of support and a music teacher's unfamiliarity with exceptional students can pave the way for failure. The director has the responsibility to provide music instruction and the right to rely on teachers' aides in instructional support roles, since students initially require the same services in both general and music education classrooms. My experience repeatedly shows that once the director becomes familiar with the student's needs and the modifications prove successful, he or she may no longer require extra support.

Administrators have an obligation to ensure proper support. For example, a building principal should endorse staggered breaks so that special education staff can assist students during music classes. I have also had cases where the principal had to alter teachers' aides' pay for after-school rehearsals. Before asking for help from administrators, directors should confer with special education colleagues to make sure that everyone agrees about the appropriateness and viability of a solution. Administrators can then make informed decisions that facilitate inclusion.

SELECTING APPROPRIATE INSTRUMENTS

Directors must take into account physical or cognitive challenges when selecting appropriate instruments for exceptional learners. Percussion instruments are possible choices for students with physical or cognitive challenges. Directors can easily modify percussion music to meet several student performance levels without reducing ensemble performance quality. You can adapt instruments and beaters so that almost every student with physical limitations can play them. Clark and Chadwick's (1980) *Clinically Adapted Instruments for the Multiply Handicapped* offers several examples of how to adapt percussion instruments and beaters, as well as solutions for adapting wind and stringed instruments.

I have had success with the two-mallet grip used primarily by keyboard percussion players (in which two mallets are held in the same hand), particularly with students with limited use of only one arm or hand (two mallets are held in the more functional hand). Professional marimba players demonstrate the independence possible with both mallets held in the hand, especially with such techniques as single-handed rolls. This grip is not limited to percussion keyboard instruments, as I have had students with limited use of one hand use this grip with almost all percussion sticks and mallets with great success. Mastering these techniques, of course, takes a good bit of practice.

Percussion instruments frequently provide solutions, but you can modify other instruments, though often less easily. Woodwind and stringed instruments require a good deal of fine motor facility, even at the beginning level. Straps can hold clarinets (some younger players use them anyway), and you can fashion holders to help secure string instruments. Stringed instruments can also be restrung to be played with opposite hands, but you should consult with an instrument repair technician first.

Brass instruments pose similar problems with embouchure formation, but some can also be played with opposite hands if finger facility is a concern. The trombone is an option if both hands have limited finger use. I had one horn student with limited use of the right hand who played the horn in the customary manner because the hand functioned adequately in the bell of the instrument, and a strap similar to those used for saxophones helped to support the instrument.

Suitable unmodified instruments often suffice for students with physical limitations. For example, students with limited finger movement may have difficulty with a woodwind or stringed instrument, but not with operating the slide of the trombone. The Moss Rehabilitation Hospital Settlement Music School Therapeutic Music Program produced *Guide to the Selection of Musical Instruments with Respect to Physical Ability and Disability* (1982). It identifies the movement that band and orchestra instruments require. Though the writing is technical and geared toward an occupational therapist, directors and trained school personnel can explore the physical movement needed to play specific instruments before making recommendations to students and parents.

Despite the realistic recommendations of the director, like typical students, exceptional learners may insist on a particular instrument.

Students may surprise directors with success in some cases, but most students quickly realize that they must consider another instrument if they have not made progress after two or three weeks.

PEERS

Respecting and valuing differences is a benefit of inclusion, but directors may need to prepare ensemble members for the arrival of the exceptional learner. Typical students can then help exceptional learners succeed.

If the student is new to the school, new to a more advanced program where students have played together for a while, or new to inclusion in that particular school, directors might consider preparing typical learners in the lesson group or ensemble for the inclusion of the new student. Directors should confer with the exceptional student if appropriate, parents, and special education staff about the best way to introduce him or her to other students, remaining sensitive to privacy issues. Because of the prevalence of inclusion in general classrooms, most students likely know exceptional needs students prior to participation in band or orchestra.

STUDENT HELPERS

Before using student helpers, remember that in beginner programs, all students new to instrumental music and must devote their full attention to their own skills. At the beginning, exceptional learners may need to have a special education teacher or aide present, but as typical students progress, a buddy might take his or her place. Typical students often assist exceptional learners they know on their own, especially in inclusive schools.

Helping exceptional peers effectively and greatly contributes to the success of typical learners as well, as they reinforce their own learning in the process, but student helpers must first have satisfactory playing skills before they assist special learners. Throughout the process, exceptional learners should not rely too heavily on their helpers to the point where they learn less on their own or restrict the development of their helpers.

LESSON AND REHEARSAL PARTICIPATION

Because I am not usually familiar with students, I schedule individual lessons with exceptional learners so I can better assess the effectiveness of any modifications. If an exceptional learner progresses at a typical rate, I move him or her into group lessons. I have had some students remain in individual lessons permanently because of their needed specialized instruction, though most of them participate in the full ensemble. For programs that have only large-group instruction, directors may want to consider individual instruction for exceptional students, at least at first. If individual instruction is not possible, a special education teacher or paraprofessional can assist the exceptional learner during large-group instruction.

I have clearly specified requirements for ensemble participation. As with typical students, if exceptional learners are capable but do not meet these expectations—most often because of a lack of home practice—they may not participate in the ensemble until they have met the necessary requirements. Obviously, instances occur where the participation requirements for exceptional learners need to be modified or waived, depending on previously identified strengths and weaknesses.

MODIFYING INSTRUCTION OR MATERIALS

Devise a plan for teaching exceptional students based on information you have already gathered. Once instruction begins and you implement your plan, assess and document progress. If exceptional learners show dedication and have an appropriate instrument but do not progress as predicted, remain open to modifying their instruction. Modifications may involve instruction sequencing or modifying music print or parts.

Task Analysis

Zdzinski (2003) recommends that teachers implement task analysis for special learners with cognitive challenges. Teachers analyze the larger task and break it down into smaller ones in planning instruction for some instrumental music students. The special education field depends heavily upon this approach, but it is also essential in teaching and learning in general. Through task analysis, learners sequentially master smaller, more achievable tasks along the way to the larger goal. Teachers generally agree that the time spent on task analysis with exceptional learners actually helps teach all learners.

For example, task analysis is usually needed to teach small children to tie shoelaces (the larger goal). Many steps (smaller goals) are required to make the double-bow knot. In the next chapter, I apply task analysis to reading notation. And though the steps I describe for introducing notation are temporary for most students, task analysis is required for almost all instruction for some of those who have cognitive challenges.

Modifications

Besides task analysis, consider your pace of instruction and how concrete your explanation and example are. You may alse need to modify music. You can simplify parts for exceptional learners and delete passages that are too difficult. These simplifications or deletions might be permanent or provide a temporary solution until learners can successfully play the part. Ensemble quality doesn't suffer if directors simplify music for some learners.

Consider color coding notation or using other visual cues. Enlarging music helps some students with cognitive challenges decode notation more easily and large-print or Braille music helps students with impaired sight. Sight-impaired students as well as several other exceptional students often learn quickly from rote learning or "playing by ear." Hearing-impaired students could require amplification devices. These are only a few examples given to illustrate the many adaptation possibilities.

Necessary modifications usually coincide with those used in students' other classes, though special education staff can help directors with any new challenges that surface specifically with instrumental music study. A growing body of literature available in professional journals and methods texts provides information about specific needs and strategies to meet these challenges in instrumental, general, and choral settings.

BEHAVIORAL CHALLENGES

Aside from physical and cognitive challenges, some students have behavioral difficulties that need attention, such as those with autism spectrum disorders. Confer with special education staff, families, and others that know the student and appropriate, effective ways of proactively creating a successful environment for him or her. Directors should also make sure they know behavior plans for a consistent approach when interventions are needed.

ADD (attention deficit disorder) and ADHD (attention deficit hyperactivity disorder) have received a good deal of attention recently. Familiar terms even outside education, ADD and ADHD create controversy because of varying opinions on causes, treatments, or if they even constitute credible disorders (Armstrong, 1999; Kunjufu, 1990). I am not an expert and will not speculate on the controversy here, but I do know that some children seem to need a higher degree of stimulation than others to stay attentive, and these students often exhibit a good deal more kinesthetic activity (movement).

Fortunately, the inherent active participation of instrumental music study is ideal for many of these students. Like typical students, they stay more engaged when well-planned lessons allow the entire ensemble to play as much as possible. Adamek and Darrow (2005) point out that students with ADD/ADHD require us to practice patience, motivate us to plan more effectively, keep us on task in the classroom, and prompt us to be more organized (p. 146). This helps us be better teachers for all students in the room.

I often keep these active or easily distracted students engaged by assigning them duties that help expedite rehearsals (such as passing out notices, music, or other managerial tasks). Clear instruction with concrete language is helpful to these learners (as well as most others). It is often wise to seat these students closer to the teacher or away from certain students who might pose conflict or distraction. When addressing off-task behavior, I use predetermined visual cues from the podium to help these students stay focused on required tasks. These nonverbal signals help minimize scrutiny by peers. Students themselves can use these signals to indicate that they need to get a drink of water or simply take a short walk up and down the hall. Of course, approach this option with caution, as students must be trusted to do this independently and only when necessary. During group lessons or even during rehearsals, I will have the entire ensemble stand (except for tubas and low strings) if I see students becoming restless. As with other exceptional learners, consult with colleagues and parents to ensure a consistent approach in addressing behavior concerns.

With proper research and preparation, directors can include most exceptional learners in their ensemble in a way that benefits all students.

Seven

Decoding Notation

How directors teach students to decode music notation (reading music) is controversial because many different strategies stem from several approaches. Regardless of method or technique, reading music notation while performing requires several tasks to be performed simultaneously.

Aside from the meanings the music symbols represent, executive skills such as bowing, breathing, tonguing, and holding the instrument also need attention at the same time. All of these many simultaneous tasks can be quite challenging for beginners.

Many directors teach reading notation and executive skills separately. Directors usually introduce executive skills necessary to play the instrument prior to notation, but revisit them only after students have formed bad habits, and experienced directors know the difficulties associated with remedying undesirable habits after they occur. Students need a sequence of instruction that helps them decode music notation but still enables a way to monitor the executive skills that playing the instrument requires.

The following sequence presents a task analysis of simultaneously playing and reading notation. Drawing on the principles of the influential Swiss educator Johann Heinrich Pestolozzi (1746–1827), this sequence allows directors "[t]o teach but one thing at a time—rhythm [and] melody . . . to be taught and practiced separately, before the child is called to the difficult task of attending to all at once" (Monroe, 1907, p. 145, as cited in Schleuter, 1997, p. 27). I analyze the larger task of reading notation while playing, divide it into five subtasks, and arrange the sequence in the following order: reading rhythm symbols, reading tonal symbols, fingering passages on the instrument, attending to playing techniques, and putting all steps together by slowly playing on the instrument.

While designing the sequence, I drew from pedagogues such as Campbell and Scott-Kassner (1995), Hamann and Gillespie (2004), Gordon (1997), Grunow and Gordon (1989), Robinson and Middleton (cited in Kohut, 1996; Middleton, Haines, & Garner, 1998), and Schleuter (1997). It should be noted that I modify these methods and techniques and use them differently than originally intended, so I encourage you to consult the cited references as well.

LEARNING SEQUENCE FOR BEGINNING INSTRUMENTAL MUSIC READING AND PLAYING

Strings

1. *Tap* basic beat (with heels of both feet with toes anchored to floor), *pat* beat divisions (with one hand on thigh while other hand holds or supports instrument), and *rap* melodic rhythm (using rhythm syllables or other counting system).
2. *Tap* basic beat (with heels), *pat* beat divisions (with one hand on thigh while the other hand holds or supports instrument), and *sing* passage (using tonal syllables or letter names).
3. *Sing* (using tonal syllables or letter names) and *finger* on instrument.
4. *Finger* on instrument and *air play* without bow (optional: grasp pencil or straw).
5. *Play* (on instrument). Repeat passage several times and gradually increase speed until secure at desired tempo.

Winds

1. *Tap* basic beat (with heels of both feet with toes anchored to floor), *pat* beat divisions (with one hand on thigh while other hand holds or supports instrument), and *rap* melodic rhythm (using rhythm syllables or other counting system).
2. *Tap* basic beat (with heels), *pat* beat divisions (with one hand on thigh), and *sing* passage (using tonal syllables or letter names).
3. *Sing* (using tonal syllables or letter names) and *finger* (trombones slide) on instrument.
4. *Finger* (trombones slide) on instrument and *air play*. (Form embouchure, tongue, and control breathing as if playing on instrument. Brass players may, at the discretion of the teacher, buzz with or without the mouthpiece instead of air playing. For all wind instruments, check for proper tonguing, articulation, and breathing.)
5. *Play* (on instrument). Repeat passage several times and gradually increase speed until secure at desired tempo.

Table 7.1 Comprehensive Sequence at a Glance

	Step 1	Step 2	Step 3	Step 4	Step 5
Strings	tap, pat, rap	tap, pat, sing	sing, finger	air play	play
Winds	tap, pat, rap	tap, pat, sing	sing, finger	air play	play
Keyboard Percussion	tap, pat, rap	tap, pat, sing	sing, finger	air play	play
Drums and Accessories	tap, pat, rap	tap, clap, rap	clap	air play	play

Keyboard Percussion

1. *Tap* basic beat (with heels of both feet with toes anchored to floor), *pat* beat divisions (with hands on thighs), and *rap* melodic rhythm (using rhythm syllables or other counting system).
2. *Tap* basic beat (with heels), *pat* beat divisions (with hands on thighs), and *sing* passage (using tonal syllables or letter names).
3. *Sing* melody (using tonal syllables or letter names) and *finger* bars on instrument with forefingers. (Sticking may be monitored here.)
4. *Air play* (play part in the air, approximating proper intervals between bars). Check for proper stroke, grip, and sticking.
5. *Play* (on instrument). Repeat passage several times and gradually increase speed until secure at desired tempo.

Drums and Accessories

1. Simultaneously *tap* basic beat (with heels of both feet with toes anchored to floor), *pat* beat divisions (with hands on thighs), and *rap* rhythm (chant using rhythm syllables or other counting system).
2. *Tap* basic beat (with heels), *clap* rhythm, and *rap* rhythm (using rhythm syllables or other counting system).
3. *Clap* rhythm.
4. *Air play* (play part in the air). Check for proper stroke, grip, and sticking.
5. *Play* (on instrument). Repeat passage several times and gradually increase speed until secure at desired tempo.

Reinforce the italicized words in the sequence to help students remember them for home practice.

RHYTHMIC FEELING

Gordon (1997), Lisk (2001), and Schleuter (1997) warn that toe-tapping is ineffective as a means of developing rhythmic accuracy. I think that some musicians at all skill levels naturally tap their feet while playing, but I concur that training all young instrumentalists to tap their feet does not help them maintain a steady pulse. Rhythm is felt kinesthetically, as Gordon (1997) points out, and Schleuter (1997) recommends large-muscle movement rather than fine motor movement such as toe-tapping to facilitate rhythmic sensation in preparatory phases of study.

Because instrumentalists are usually seated, Schleuter (1997) recommends that children respond to "tempo-beat" feeling while sitting "by keeping the toe anchored and raising the heel off the floor" (p. 83), which is large-muscle movement. I adopted this movement during the first two steps of the sequence for both sitting and standing (percussion and string bass) players, but you might notice that I do not include this "heel-tapping" in the steps involving the instrument. Large-muscle movement aims to help students sense rhythm, not train them to move their feet while playing.

Having students pat the beat divisions (such as eighth notes) on the thighs further helps students to feel a steady basic beat. It also prepares beginners to accurately perform beat divisions and subdivisions (such as sixteenth notes).

A CONSISTENT COUNTING SYSTEM

The five-step sequence above accommodates the use of either developmental rhythm syllables or a counting system. I have used rhythm syllables such as those associated with Music Learning Theory (developed by Edwin Gordon and others) and with Kodály approaches with success and endorse their use. However, these and other well-known systems are most effective if used consistently over a long period of time. In my school district and many others, student transience is quite common, and often no uniform rhythm syllable system is used so that students have instructional consistency when changing schools. Further, I start older beginners in higher grades throughout the school year and must get them caught up to their peers quickly. Consequently, I now use the counting system adopted as standard in the United States ("1, and, 2, e, ah," etc.) near the beginning of instruction but use a unique system to help students feel duration.

When training students to be accomplished performers, frequent, regular drill with a logical sequence of rhythms is necessary. In order to facilitate accurate performance of varied rhythms, students must learn a consistent counting system. A consistent system is a critical piece missing in instruction in many programs, particularly in large school districts with several music teachers and as many teaching methods. Although you may not be able to institute a universal counting system that spans the entire music development of your students, you can implement a consistent system that will make up for any lapses in prior instruction and help them perform rhythms accurately while studying music with you.

Developmental Rhythm Syllables

As mentioned earlier, many approaches advocate that students in the primary grades learn developmental speech rhythms or rhythm syllables (e. g., "du du-day" or "ta ti-ti"). Later, when instrumental music study begins, many American students are then taught the counting system most commonly used, consisting of numbers and syllables representing divisions (usually eighth notes) and subdivisions (usually sixteenth notes) of beat units such as *one, two-and, three-e-and-ah, four*. The developmental rhythm systems enable students to audiate or hear rhythm in the mind before they are asked to count rhythms with an understanding of the music theory of meter or time signature, beat units per measure, and so on (Gordon, 1997).

I advocate the progression of developmental rhythm syllables before counting systems. Unfortunately many districts have multiple teachers using several approaches and methods, so consistency is rare. As mentioned earlier, I also have a revolving enrollment where students begin instrumental music study at multiple grades and skill levels. To teach all experience and skill levels simultaneously, I must forgo developmental rhythm syllables. Because the counting system used in the following figures is the most common in the United States, I teach this system so my students, many of whom will continue music in multiple schools and districts, are prepared for further study after leaving my program.

Speech Rhythms

As mentioned earlier, instrumental music programs can be designed to start beginners at all grade levels. My multi-age beginners first decode rhythm notation through speech rhythms, which we call "rhythm rapping." I use food names that correspond consistently to rhythms (see Figure 7.1), though you can use any words as long as they are consistently paired with specific rhythms. Students enjoy generating their own too. The same speech rhythms for note values are used for corresponding rests, but rests are whispered instead of chanted with full voice.

(Whisper)

Chant: "Beet   Sal-ad   Brocc-o-li   Caul-i-flow-er   Beet   Ex----tra Cu--cumb-er   Ra-dish-es   Carr------ots"

Figure 7.1   Speech rhythms

When students are rapping rhythms accurately after a couple months of study, I introduce beat grouping within measures so that a counting system makes sense to them. However, even after introducing the counting system, new rhythms are first rapped with speech rhythms until secure—usually a week or two depending on lesson or rehearsal frequency—before using the counting system with the new rhythms.

Developing Beat Feeling and Steady Pulse

As mentioned earlier, many noted pedagogues agree that teaching students to tap their feet while playing is ineffective. However, heel tapping (gross motor movement) better instills beat feeling, and simultaneously dividing the beat by patting hands on thighs helps maintain a steady pulse. For example, in common time, students will tap the quarter notes with both heels while tapping eighth notes with one hand on the thigh, while the other hand holds the instrument (Figure 7.2). In triple meter such as 6/8, students tap heels on the dotted quarter notes and divide three eighth notes per beat with one hand on the thigh.

Though I seldom find it necessary to have students divide the beat further than two or three divisions, students can also tap subdivisions (e. g., sixteenth notes in common time) with the hands on thighs while chanting tricky rhythms with sixteenth notes. Students can alternate between both hands for very rapid subdivisions, but keep the hand used for beat divisions the same, usually determined by left- or right-handedness, and add the weaker hand for the subdivisions (*e's* and *ah's*). Of course, be sure instruments are secure before using both hands!

Teaching Precise Duration

Many teachers have students emphasize or accent the beginning of durations while also verbally counting subdivisions (Figure 7.3). But some students then accent the beginnings of notes and also audibly subdivide notes with breath, sticks or mallets, or bows while playing. My students do not accent the beginning of notes when counting for this reason. Further, they do not subdivide eighth notes with their voices because they are already subdividing with their hands on thighs. This alleviates unwanted accents while playing.

The following movement should accompany all rhythm chanting.

Figure 7.2   Establishing beat feeling and steady pulse

Figure 7.3   Incorrect counting technique with accents

Because of the movement of heels and hands it is not necessary to verbally divide or subdivide using my system, rhythm is organized around the beat (at least in Western European music styles) and students must be aware of beat numbers and feel where they fall, particularly as rhythms become more difficult. Because students must be aware of the placements of beats even though all beats will not be articulated, have students count all beat numbers, but remove the first letter of beats that are "inside" durations (see Figure 7.4) so that those beat numbers begin with a vowel sound. For example, a half note in common time would be counted: "One, 'wo (pronounced "oo")." A whole note would be counted: "One, 'wo ("oo"), 'ree, 'our (pronounced "or")." Because all beats are counted, a dotted quarter note at the beginning of the measure in common time would be counted: "One, 'wo, and." Although all beat numbers are counted, removing the first consonants of beat numbers within durations leaves a fluid vowel sound that approximates what air and tongue, sticks and mallets, and bows will do when performing rhythms on an instrument.

Some directors have students count rests silently. However, experience has shown that students must count rests aloud with other rhythms for greater accuracy. All rests in my method are counted as notes are but whispered (see Figure 7.4). For example, a whole note rest in common time is counted the same as a whole note, but students whisper the four beats instead. Rhythmic accuracy is greater if students make a distinction between sound and silence encoded in rhythmic notation by vocalizing note durations at full voice (at appropriate dynamic level markings if included in rhythm patterns) and whispering rests.

1. Remove first consonants of beat numbers that are included in durations.
2. Rests are counted the same as notes, but whispered instead of full voice.
3. Students tap heels on beat and tap divisions (eighth-notes) with hands on thighs

Figure 7.4   Correct counting technique emphasizing duration properly

Triple Meter

There are many versions of counting rhythms in triple meter. With 6/8, 12/8, and so on confusion can arise because the notation and common counting system is similar to duple even though rhythm is felt differently in triple meter because of three subdivisions per beat. Again, help students feel this rhythmic change from duple to triple with the three divisions per beat they perform with hands on thighs in triple meter (see Figure 7.2, measure 3).

A common challenge students encounter is when duple and triple meter appear in the same rhythmic passage. If the change is extended, there will be a meter change, of course. But students usually encounter miniature meter changes first through triplet rhythms. Because triplets are most often introduced in duple meters, a distinction needs to be made between duple divisions (typically two eighth notes) and triplet subdivisions (three eighth notes) while counting. When learning to perform triplets, my students will change from two- to three-beat divisions with their hands on thighs during the duration of the triplet while keeping a consistent beat with their heels. After the triplet figure(s), students return to two eighth note divisions with the hands (Figure 7.5).

Some directors have students count triplet using common duple meter counting syllables (e.g., "1-and-ah, 2-and-ah"). But confusion results because the triplets have a different rhythmic feel (three to a beat), so should be counted differently. Therefore, have students continue to count beats with numbers on the first eighth note of the triplet, but the other two eighth notes are counted with "trip" and "let" (Figure 7.5). Counting numbers and syllables for some advanced triplet rhythms as well as some asymmetrical division and subdivisions are shown in Figure 7.6.

I encourage you to study methods associated with Music Learning Theory written by Gordon (1997), Grunow and Gordon (1989), Schleuter (1997), and many others, as well as approaches developed by pedagogues such as Kodály, Orff, and Dalcroze to see how they may be incorporated in how you teach rhythm notation reading. However,

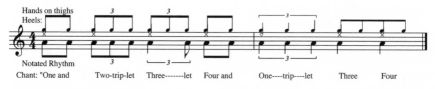

Figure 7.5 Triplets

Figure 7.6 Some advanced rhythms

regardless of chosen pedagogy, a consistent, commonly used counting system together with a method that fosters rhythmic accuracy and steady pulse, along with frequent opportunities to read and perform logically sequenced rhythms, will enable all students to become accomplished rhythm readers.

SINGING AND PITCH

Singing is integral to the learning sequence because instrumental music students often learn most efficiently when they first attempt skills through the most natural instrument: the voice. Among other things, incorporating singing activities helps students develop a sense of tonality, musical phrasing, and style of articulation. Further, virtually all music teachers agree that the ability to sing pitches facilitates proper tuning and intonation. You can monitor pitch accuracy when students sing in steps 2 and 3 for strings, winds, and keyboard percussion.

Acquiring musical understanding is facilitated by audiation, defined as hearing and comprehending in the mind musical sound that is not merely memorized or imitated. Gordon (1997) extols the importance of singing in realizing audiation: "To audiate a melody, students must be able to sing, because when they engage in tonal audiation they unconsciously sing silently" (p. 37). He advocates singing solfège syllables because they help students understand the syntax of typical tonal patterns (in Western music, that is) such as the dominant function of *so* and *ti* typically resolving to *do* at cadences.

I endorse the moveable *do–la*-based minor solfège system (Gordon, 1997; see also Grunow & Gordon, 1989; Schleuter, 1997) to foster an understanding of Western musical syntax. You can use it consistently across various grade levels and music classes (general music, choir, orchestra, and band). But because of specific issues that affect my program, I have had to adapt a different solfège system for pitches. Although I hesitated to tinker with established methods at first, I am now certain it is necessary to adapt methods and techniques to work effectively in the varying conditions of instrumental music programs.

Established methods that assume a consistent approach over several years are not realistic in some situations. For example, many directors face multiple feeder schools and student transience, particularly in large urban districts, and the consistency of instruction suffers. Additionally, the amount of time I have and the instructional goals I desire for my program usually mean that I must distil, adapt, or meld existing methods and techniques. I also created my own methods as I did with pitch names.

Band instruments present transposing issues, and students need consistent "concert pitch" syllables for singing when using the notation reading sequence. As an example of adapting established techniques, I teach solfège syllables with a fixed *do* on concert B-flat and a *do*-based minor for singing (which requires the use of different solfège syllables such as the flatted third and sixth). Dalcroze and other European pedagogues advocate this system, but they use C as *do* (the most familiar key for pianists), aiming to acquire perfect pitch (Landis & Carder, 1990, p. 20). However, B-flat is the most familiar key for wind instruments in band programs, particularly for those using most current method books. I use a fixed B-flat–*do* system simply as a matter of practicality within ever-increasing time constraints.

I attach the letter name to pitches as Grunow and Gordon (1989) endorse. For example, with instruments in concert pitch, the pitches of the B-flat major scale would be referred to as B-flat–*do*, C–*re*, D–*mi*, E-flat–*fa*, and so on; for instruments that transpose, such as clarinets and trumpets, the same pitches are referred to as C–*do*, D–*re*, E–*mi*, F–*fa*, and so on. In this system, all students sing the same tonal syllable regardless of instrument transposition by omitting the letter name while singing, but they still learn the universal letter names specific to instrument transposition.

Given a unison passage, students can thus sing the same solfège syllables and pitches and alleviate confusion with transposition in heterogeneous group lessons and rehearsals. When students leave for other programs, they know the universal letter names already and easily adapt to new solfège systems, if necessary.

Again, I use the stationary *do* system for practical reasons. If using B-flat concert as stationary *do*, B-flat is always *do*, regardless of key. Further, this method means that all pitches, solfège syllables, and letter names remain the same regardless of key. Students consistently refer to the same solfège syllables and pitches with the same fingerings or slide positions.

Using the stationary *do* system helps reduce performance errors. For example, beginning band students often confuse the pitch A with the pitch Ab concert (especially when learning the key of E-flat major after Bb major). With stationary do, A–*ti* in B-flat major becomes A-flat–*te* in E-flat major. The combined pitch, letter, and fingering/slide change (A–*ti* to Ab–*te*) helps students remember the new pitch in E-flat major.

In the previous sequence, students sing a different solfège syllable as they change fingering or slide positions, thus pairing the aural change (*ti* to *te*) with the kinesthetic change of fingering or slide position (concert A to A-flat). This aural-kinesthetic clarity is important when students change keys and when accidentals appear in familiar keys.

Though critics may argue that ample audiation training makes aural-kinesthetic association unnecessary, the audiation techniques they offer often assume dated instrumental music program designs that are increasingly rare in the present day, such as the assumption that students begin together at the beginning of the school year and remain together for subsequent years. Solfège syllables with stationary *do* work well with many exceptional needs students, those with limited musical ability, in situations where limited time is available for instruction, and when students enter programs at various times.

In my opinion, solfège syllables provide the best but not the only option. You can use letter names, particularly with strings. They are in concert pitch, and students sing the same letter names regardless of instrument grouping. However, when working on unison passages in heterogeneous settings with transposing instruments, such as full orchestra or band ensembles, students sing different letter names. Students grow accustomed to this, and it should not pose a significant distraction if you use the sequence regularly.

EXECUTIVE SKILLS

Playing techniques such as posture and hand and finger placement can be monitored in the sequence. I designed the fourth step primarily for the reinforcement of technique. For example, this step for winds ("finger and air play") very effectively prevents wind students from breathing after every note, which beginners commonly do. Air playing, or forming the embouchure, tonguing, and controlling breathing as if playing while fingering the instrument, allows teachers to monitor when students take breaths.

You can effectively observe proper tonguing or its absence, as in the case of slurring. I usually have brass players buzz into mouthpieces while fingering during this step. In large groups, this buzzing may overpower the sound of woodwind air players, so brass players must air play with lips slightly parted. Trombone players slide instead of fingering, of course, but they must air play by buzzing the lips away from the mouthpiece while sliding, or buzz into the mouthpiece while approximating slide positions in the air without the instrument, due to the way it must be held while playing. Even with these necessary modifications, the step is still effective for young trombonists.

Air playing effectively improves precise entrances (attacks) and releases. In my experience, uniform releases pose more of a problem than uniform entrances, and air playing effectively monitors them. With more problematic releases, modifying the Breath Rhythmic Impulse Method (BRIM), first developed by Robinson and Middleton (Kohut, 1996; Middleton, Haines, & Garner, 1998), can help. I have wind students pulse

Chapter Seven

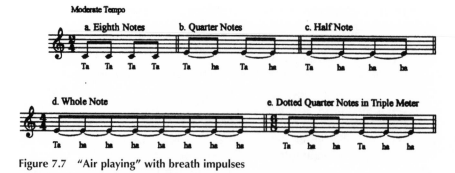

Figure 7.7 "Air playing" with breath impulses

beat subdivisions using the diaphragm, much like the common technique used for teaching diaphragm vibrato. For example, when a half note receives two beats at a moderate tempo, students would subdivide into four eighth notes and say "ta ha ha ha" while air playing (see Figure 7.7). Students and I call breath impulses "pushes." Air playing with "pushes" helps students feel exactly how long to sustain the tone and release it without being encumbered by the instrument.

The BRIM technique is an excellent way to coordinate where to take breaths. Most wind players have difficulty coordinating the release of the tone and intake of air at the ends of phrases properly while maintaining a steady pulse, and they "breathe with the beat" instead. For example, they play a half note at the end of a phrase for only one beat and breathe on the second beat instead of sustaining the tone. Subdividing durations with breath impulses ("pushes") coordinates phrasing and breathing for wind students at all skill levels.

Wind players should use breath impulses frequently at first so that students become accustomed to the technique. They can do "pushes" while playing the instrument, but I usually have students do them only while air playing. Again, as with the Gordon method, I strayed from Middleton's original BRIM technique to serve my own goal of honing uniform durations and releases. Middleton's method has benefits beyond my purposes if used consistently and in the manner he intended. If you are unfamiliar with them, I encourage you to read further about Gordon's and Middleton's methods and techniques, as well as those developed by the other pedagogues cited, and see if you can incorporate them more fully in your practice.

At the beginning stages of instruction or when you introduce new bowing techniques, strings should air play and demonstrate proper grip, hand, and arm motion by simulating bow gestures (without the bow) while still fingering the strings with the left hand. To assist proper bow grip formation, students may hold pencils; to encourage a relaxed grip, students can hold straws, which bend if they apply too much pressure

(Hamann & Gillespie, 2004, p. 50). Air playing for strings helps to check executive bowing skills without the encumbrance of the bow's weight.

For keyboard percussion, "sing and finger" encourages students to keep their eyes on the music while using peripheral vision to find the bars of the instrument, an often-neglected skill necessary for successfully reading notation for the keyboard percussion instruments. Other common problems include proper sticking, grip, and stroke. Through air play, you can monitor the mallet and drums or accessories. The relaxed stroke and rebound used while playing in the air is similar to the desired technique for striking percussion instruments, and particularly benefits stroke development.

WHEN TO USE THE SEQUENCE

Use this sequence when you first introduce music notation or when encountering problematic passages. The learning sequence is effective for short (four- to eight-measure) songs or passages. Providing a means to remedy problems during home practice is a crucial component of properly training students; so teach this sequence for school use as well as home practice.

Even though this method is for introducing notation, "rote before note" or "sound before symbol" methods still apply when considering best practice for beginners. The first pitches, meters, and rhythms included as part of many method books are best introduced through movement activities, rote learning (imitating the teacher), and playing by ear, all of which should precede reading notation and the sequence presented here. All my students play by rote and by ear exclusively the first couple of weeks and continue later in the form of improvisation. Contrary to some established methods, I cannot use these activities for extensive periods because of time constraints.

Notice that the learning sequence consists of five steps for all instruments and that I modify and correlate them to instruments found in typical beginner ensembles. You can use the sequence for both mixed group and homogeneous lessons or rehearsals.

OMITTING AND ISOLATING STEPS

Although you should use the sequence when students first learn to read, remember that students join band and orchestra to play instruments, not to sing and chant. Furthermore, they cannot rely on this sequence indefinitely. As teachers note progress, they should monitor students to see if they read and perform proficiently enough to omit all or part of the sequence. After the first couple of weeks of reading (or even sooner with older beginners), see if students can read songs or passages without the sequence. It serves little purpose (and students find the process boring) if they must use it with familiar music that they already play well or with music they can read easily.

You need not use the sequence in its entirety. For example, you can obviously omit step 3 ("sing and finger") for stringed instruments during the open strings stages and add it when introducing fingering. Air bowing in step 4 is useful for teaching basic bow techniques needed before introducing notation.

As students become more proficient at playing and reading, you can gradually omit steps, depending on the problems you observe. For example, with a few weeks of experience, wind players can probably articulate properly with the tongue without breathing after every note, so you can omit air play until an articulation, breathing, or release problem occurs again. As students gain more experience reading but later encounter an unfamiliar or problematic passage, abbreviate the sequence to only include the "tap, pat, and rap" and "sing and finger" steps for strings, winds, and keyboard percussion, and the "tap, pat, and rap" and "clap" steps for drums.

You can isolate steps to remedy problems with more advanced students. Quite possibly, only one aspect of student performance is weak when performing a given passage. Directors can isolate a step to address the problem and see if the passage improves when played again. For example, if the pitches were played correctly with the proper articulation but the rhythm was inaccurate, students can "tap, pat, and rap" (step 1) the rhythm of the passage and see if rhythmic accuracy improves. After students have read notation for a few weeks, this process of diagnosing and remedying problems with isolated steps in the sequence saves precious time and maintains student interest in the rehearsal or lesson.

SOME TIPS FOR SUCCESSFUL IMPLEMENTATION

To help younger students understand the sequence, change terminology to better describe basic beats and beat divisions, such as "big beats" (with the heels) and "little beats" (with the hands on the lap). Some students have trouble coordinating these two movements at first, but tapping basic beats with the heels while patting beat divisions on the thigh aids accurate performance of rhythm patterns and steady pulse maintenance, a common problem with young players. If coordination is a problem, have students get the "big beats" first and then add the "little beats" after the "big beats" are secure. Then students may proceed with the rest of the given step (rapping rhythms or singing). Most students gradually improve their coordination with simultaneous heel movement (basic beats) and lap patting (beat divisions) by using this process consistently over time.

I use heel-tapping for all instruments because it is a large-muscle move-ment appropriate for students seated in close proximity and even for per-cussionists and string bassists, who typically stand. Other movements are also effective, such as swaying the upper body back and forth in response to the basic beats while still patting the beat divisions on the thighs. You can vary movements to feel both basic beats and beat divisions to add variety and maintain interest, particularly with younger students.

Despite all the positive results attributed to singing, some teachers prefer that students not sing passages before playing them. I believe that this hesitancy may sometimes stem from the directors' unease with singing themselves, but they often argue that if a student sings passages incorrectly, confusion results when played pitches differ from sung ones. The possibility of a real detriment seems remote when this occurs, and the benefits of singing outweigh any temporary confusion caused by a possible discrepancy between passages. Providing many opportunities to sing during instruction at school improves pitch accuracy at home.

Most band method publishers also offer accompaniments and playing exemplars on compact disc that students may use at home to help them sing and play accurately. Some publishers even offer free CDs and access to websites where students can download accompaniments and other aids. When using the recordings, students hear correct pitches and a con-sistent beat that helps them as they use the sequence at home. They can play along with the recording after they have performed all the steps in the sequence to check their performance accuracy.

EXCEPTIONAL LEARNERS

Many exceptional learners find the sequence helpful and may only require slight modification. For students with more pronounced cogni-tive challenges, you may need to break these steps down further, and some exceptional learners need to use the sequence longer than typical students. This sequence is also effective with English language learners because no knowledge of English is required (except number names for counting which are learned immediately). All teacher demonstration and student performance is done through movement, counting or tonal syl-lables, and chanting and singing within the context of music.

The sequence also helps students who may not have intervention services but may trail behind peers when decoding notation symbols. Students who fear failure and give up easily have particular success with this sequence, and the better notation readers remain engaged when repeating the sequence a few extra times for those struggling. If some students continue struggling to read notation after the first few weeks, other techniques (as well as a possible lesson group change, if possible) may need to be considered. Typical students grow tired of the sequence when they don't need it.

Reinforcing good musical habits early improves performance, skills, and overall enjoyment in both the long and short run. Break the rules a little bit and try modifying established methods that are practical to use in your classrooms.

Eight

Improvisation and Composition

Most music educators agree that the creative activities of improvisation and composition are components of a complete music education. According to the MENC National Standards, "The curriculum for every student should include improvisation and composition. Many students gain considerable information about music and acquire rudimentary performing skills, but too few have ample opportunities to improvise and compose music" (MENC, 1994, p. 4). You can, however, include improvisation and composition even in rehearsals with very limited time. Using an efficient method is the key.

Like performance, improvising and composing have varied skill levels, but every student can engage in these activities to a certain extent. Some music educators argue that limited opportunities to try such skills contribute to why we have so few improvisers and composers. Increased exposure dispels the sense of mystery and apprehension often associated with improvisation and composition. Unfortunately, directors' inexperience and the demand to prepare for performances limit students' opportunities to pursue these creative endeavors.

A great deal of the improvisational resources available centers on jazz. Composition teaching techniques come from the general music realm and may have limited application in instrumental music classes. Yet by adapting some of these existing techniques, as well as designing others specifically for instrumental ensembles, you can introduce creative, expressive activities that expose students at all levels to improvisation and composition while actually reinforcing performance goals. Thus, the time spent learning how to improvise and compose does not detract from building performance skills. Indeed, if designed and implemented correctly, the two creative endeavors actually strengthen students' performance ability.

IMPROVISATION

Jazz (and even Western European or so-called classical music) has always relied on improvisation. Because of this prevalence in music throughout the world, a comprehensive instrumental music education simply should include improvisation activities. Elliot (1995), in his philosophical treatise *Music Matters*, feels strongly enough about the importance of improvising to assert that "performing and improvising (when improvising is germane to a practice) ought to be the foundational and primary forms of music making taught and learned in music education programs" (p. 172). Unfortunately, while students learn to perform in instrumental music classes, they are rarely taught to improvise.

Some directors feel that instrumental music classes have too little time to teach improvisation because of performance demands. However, a research study by Azzara (1993) found a correlation between beginning students who engage in improvisation and an increased ability to perform while reading notation.

Good improvisers play by ear proficiently. Some musicians, particularly in non-Western and jazz styles, prize "ear playing" and have little or no need for notation. Interestingly, McPherson and Gabrielsson (2002) conclude that ear playing as a pre-notation activity actually helps students better understand notation.

Most directors realize the depth of study required to improvise in the jazz style and naturally conclude that only jazz students should learn improvisation. True, traditional methods of teaching jazz improvisation are not often easily adapted for several music genres at various skill levels (though improvising in multiple genres and skill levels helps students learn jazz improvisation). For this reason, while drawing on the work of eminent pedagogues such as Azzara, Grunow, and Gordon (1997), Azzara and Grunow (2006), Gordon (1997), Grunow and Gordon (1989), and Schleuter (1997), I developed a method to teach students in large ensemble groups how to improvise quickly with limited instruction time. My sequence is consistent with Music Learning Theory approaches (see treatise on "bridging" in Bluestine, 2000, p. 165), though it should be noted that the method and, to some extent, the function of rhythm and tonal syllables is significantly different. However, in a few minutes during rehearsal or lessons, this sequence taps into students' creative abilities, helps them play by ear, improves reading skill, and serves as warm-up exercises at the beginning of rehearsals or lessons.

IMPROVISATION SEQUENCE

Rhythm Sequence

1. Start with rote activity: You chant a neutral syllable ("lu"), and students echo. After students echo your four-beat rhythm without pausing, insert a four-beat rest before you chant the next rhythm (see Figure 8.1). Keeping this four-beat rest consistent throughout the sequence helps students improvise in step 5.
2. Add rhythm syllables or another counting system. You chant using rhythm syllables ("du" or "ta" for quarter notes) or a counting system, and students echo. Note: I have students softly say "mmm" for the duration of all rests, as rests move, but quietly.
3. You chant on neutral syllable ("lu"), and students chant back using rhythm syllables or the counting system. You can monitor students to see if they audiate the rhythm patterns rather than merely echo back the rhythm in rote fashion. To correct errors, chant the rhythm back with students after they have tried to chant it on their own. If errors still occur after several corrections, begin the sequence again, as students may not be ready for this step.
4. You sing on a comfortable playing note using pitch name, and students sing rhythm back on the same pitch. I begin with concert D–*mi* with band students (as notated in Figure 8.1), one of the first and easiest unison pitches my students learn. This step allows students to sing the rhythm accurately before adding the skills necessary to play it on the instrument.
5. You sing a neutral syllable or play rhythm pattern, and students play back (such as on D–*mi*).
6. Individual students improvise rhythm patterns, and the rest of class plays back. Students take turns improvising in a call-and-response manner. You should demonstrate a few patterns and take volunteers at first, and then point to any student during the four-beat rest between each call and response. Students have the option to "pass," but they all should become willing participants with experience.

Note: For steps 1 through 4 above, students should tap basic beats with the heels and pat beat divisions with one hand on thigh as described in the previous chapter.

(Rest four beats before beginning next pattern.)

Figure 8.1   Beginning rhythm pattern example

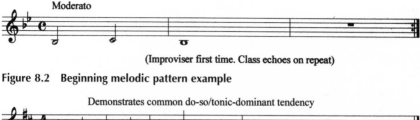

(Improviser first time. Class echoes on repeat)

Figure 8.2   Beginning melodic pattern example

(Improviser first time. Class echoes on repeat)

Figure 8.3   More advanced melodic pattern example

Melody Sequence

1. You sing on a neutral syllable ("lu"), and students echo. Start with only two pitches and very simple rhythms at a slow to moderate tempo. Be sure to include the rest after each pattern (see figures 8.2 and 8.3).
2. You sing syllables (*do, re, mi,* or letter names), and students echo.
3. You sing pattern on a neutral syllable, and students sing back the pattern using pitch names. At first, give the starting pitch name to students during the rest at the end of the melody to get them started. They will make a few mistakes at first, every time you add a new pitch; students must audiate before responding. To correct these errors, sing the melody back with students after they have tried to sing it on their own. This method of correcting errors as they occur becomes a game as students become increasingly motivated to sing the pattern correctly and check their accuracy in the "sing back" with the teacher. Omit the "sing back" with the teacher if students respond with the correct pitch names. If errors still occur after several "sing backs," begin the sequence again as students may not be ready for this step.
4. You sing on neutral syllable or—better yet—play a melodic pattern, and students play back. Similar to the error correction in step 3, if you hear errors, sing the melody with pitch names after students have attempted to play the pattern by themselves.
5. An individual student plays, and the rest of the group plays back in call-and-response fashion. You should demonstrate a few patterns and ask for volunteers at first, and then later simply point to students during the rest between patterns.

USING THE SEQUENCE

Not only does this sequence help students start improvising, but the first steps of this sequence constitute rote or ear-playing activities that you use before beginning students are ready to play together. In my first couple of years of teaching, I would not begin rehearsals for a month or two after lessons began to allow students time to gain the necessary skills to play together in unison. Now I can begin rehearsals concurrently with lessons. In programs without lesson or small-group instruction, this improvisation sequence can be used during the very first rehearsals.

Steps 1 through 4 of the rhythm sequence and steps 1 through 3 of the melodic sequence are appropriate even before students can play instruments together because they do not involve playing. I find that the reading accuracy of both rhythms and pitches improves when students are introduced to them through improvisation first.

To help the success of younger players, this improvisation sequence also initially isolates rhythm and pitch. I begin with four-beat quarter note/quarter rest rhythms (see Figure 8.1), and add more complex rhythms as the year progresses. New pitches also adhere to this idea of gradual complexity. To save time, introduce new pitches in individual or group lessons, if possible, because of the extra time needed to learn new fingerings and other executive skills.

Students need not use the entire sequence every time they improvise. Instead, progress through each step in the sequence only when learning new rhythms (eighth notes or dotted quarter/eighth notes, for example) or when learning new pitches.

It is not necessary for every student to demonstrate proficiency before moving on. Move your group to the next step in the sequence "when about 80 percent of the class can do the patterns correctly. This is another of Gordon's suggestions [as part of the Music Learning Theory approach], and I like it" (Bluestine, 2000, p. 199). Make a point to review steps in the sequence in subsequent rehearsals for students who are struggling. Considering limited time, I find that approximately six typical melodies or rhythms are sufficient for the easier steps. For example, with *do* and *re* melodies, directors may begin with *do–re–do*, *re–do–re*, *do–do–re*, *re–re–do*, *do–re–re*, and *re–do–do*, using the rhythms in Figure 8.2. Students will require more patterns at steps requiring audiation (step 3 in the rhythm sequence and steps 3 through 5 in the melodic sequence). Be sure student performance is accurate at each step before moving on to the next one.

Steps 1, 2, 4, and 5 with rhythms should only take a couple of minutes each, and steps 3 and 6 should take 5 to 10 minutes. I have found that students have more difficulty with melodies than rhythms, so steps 3 through 5 may each take a rehearsal or lesson session of 5 or 10 minutes at first. All steps do not need to occur in a single session. For example, one rehearsal may involve only steps 1 and 2. The next rehearsal might begin with a quick review of the first two steps using the same melodies and the addition of step 3.

As students get used to improvising, these steps take even less time and become seamless. After a month with rehearsals meeting two to three times weekly, I can introduce a new rhythm or pitch using the entire sequence in only one 5- to 10-minute rehearsal session. Rehearsal time can be maximized even further if you structure the rhythms and melodies to replace warm-ups. For example, rapid rhythm improvisations can serve to get tongues, fingers, and bows moving, while melodies with longer durations can serve as long tones and intonation exercises.

Limiting choices ensures success with rhythms and beginning improvisation. Gradually add more pitches and more complex rhythms as students gain proficiency. I start with two pitches, preferably before students have seen them in notation, and use the same half note–half note–whole note–whole rest rhythm (see Figure 8.2) for several weeks, even though I may add three or four additional notes. As mentioned earlier, I find that students struggle with melodies more than rhythms, so I keep the melodic rhythms simple and consistent.

The whole rest at the end of melodies (see Figures 8.2 and 8.3) is important because it gives students the extra time needed to audiate them. In other words, students have time to process what they have heard into pitches or syllables and, later in the sequence, into pitches that they can play. This rest between improviser and group is not necessary with the rhythm sequence (compare rhythm sequence Figure 8.1 to melody sequence Figure 8.2).

It helps if students know solfège syllables, particularly in band, because the many letter names for transposing instruments are a little confusing (though certainly not impossible). For ease in improvisation activities, I teach the combination of letter and solfège names advocated by Grunow and Gordon (1989). For example, B-flat–*do*, C–*re*, and D–*mi* are used for concert pitched instruments; C–*do*, D–*re*, E–*mi* for B-flat instruments; G–*do*, A–*re*, B–*mi* for E-flat instruments, and so on. In mixed group settings, we easily refer to pitch names simply as *do, re, mi*, omitting the pitch letter name at the beginning.

As previously discussed, Gordon advocates the use of movable *do* (where solfège syllables change with tonality), and directors should consider this technique first. Because of my program structure and the time allowed for beginning instruction, I have had more success with immovable or stationary *do*, where the solfège syllables remain the same regardless of tonality.

BEYOND THE BEGINNING STAGE

Separating rhythm and melody for improvisation becomes much less crucial as students gain experience with melodies. When directors introduce new or complex rhythms, melodies should remain simple, and new pitches and complex melodies should have simple rhythms.

Though a few new pitches and rhythms provide the context for improvisation experiences at first, improvisation can expand to include entire major and minor scales as students progress. Soon after the beginning stages, you should help students understand the commonly accepted syntax of pitch intervals within melodies. For example, you can discuss the leading tone's tendency to move to the tonic, the static quality of the tonic, the tonic–dominant relationship, and so on (see Figure 8.3).

Gordon (1997) uses the clarification of interval relationships as a rationale for using movable *do*, because regardless of key, *ti* or *sol* typically resolves to *do*, *re* resolves to *do* or *mi*, and so on. However, in the stationary *do* system, I illustrate these tonal tendencies in the key of B-flat, the initial key that my band students learn. Thus, the first scale degree is *do*, the dominant is *sol*, and so on. Because *do* is concert B-flat regardless of key, I ensure that students understand scale degrees and can refer to *mi* as the third, *sol* as the fifth, and so on.

I later apply these interval relationships to other keys and refer to intervals by number, as traditionally done when discussing music theory. For example, I tell students that, in the key of E-flat, *te* (concert A-flat) is the fourth, and *do* (concert B-flat) is the fifth. Regardless of whether you use stationary or movable *do* systems, point out common interval tendencies to help student improvisations develop from mere random pitch or rhythm selection into communicative, expressive improvisation.

Understanding harmonic structure is fundamental to generating meaningful improvisation. Soon after learning the first scales, introduce harmony using the sequence for melodies. Students can improvise and echo using root, third (major or minor), and fifth, or the ensemble can sustain first and fifth scale degrees (sometimes referred to as drones) or triads (first, third, and fifth scale degrees) while a soloist improvises scale patterns. Certain scale degrees sound better than others, and with your guidance students quickly discover what pitches they think fit best. After harmonic structure, introduce the concept of harmonic progression by having individual students improvise over chord roots of simple harmonic progressions played by the ensemble (see Azzara & Grunow, 2006; Azzara, Grunow, & Gordon, 1997).

After triads and harmonic progressions, introduce sevenths, and students are on the way to jazz improvisation. With respect to the traditional jazz style, I find that the rhythm sequence helps to teach students to swing eighth notes. Directors may also use the melody sequence with the blues scale and scale modes, beginning with the first two or three scale degrees and adding pitches as students demonstrate proficiency.

In designing this sequence, I accounted for the development of beginning improvisers as well as advanced students while also allowing for the limited time usually devoted to rehearsals. Consequently, I can improvise with my beginning groups using only about 5 minutes each rehearsal. Not only do I provide students with a more complete instrumental music education, but also my students feel that improvisation is one of the most enjoyable parts of their instrumental music experience.

Composition

Reimer (1989) feels that "while some degree of progress has been made in recent years toward effective methods of involving students in musical composition, this aspect of music education . . . remains a major piece of unfinished business for the profession" (p. 71). Part of the problem is that so many resources on how to teach composition, how students compose, and appropriate composition activities are geared only to the general or classroom setting. Further, preparing music for performance becomes the top priority. Directors can, however, design composition activities that still reinforce performance goals.

The "degree of progress" in student compositions to which Reimer refers is partly due to the advent of computer technology and software devoted to music notation and playback. Directors save valuable time designing composition activities using the computer. Once designed, you can save these activities for years to come. Using the computer for student composition is probably most appropriate for general music instruction or in instrumental music programs where students have sufficient time and ample access to computers and necessary software. Regardless of access to computer technology, composing by hand first has advantages similar to writing letters and words before learning to type.

Although a computer can render a performance simulation in classroom music settings, using live musicians is more instructive and satisfying. Elliott (1995) feels that "[m]usic is a performing art. The intended outcome or work in the performing arts is not a self-sufficient object (like painting, novel, or sculpture) but rather a performance" (p. 172). Instrumental music ensembles provide this opportunity to both create and perform.

Playback features available with notation software render sterile and inaccurate virtual performances. Students need to learn instrument ranges, abilities of live players, transpositions, and so on. Virtually every book on composing, arranging, and orchestration recommends performance of compositions by live musicians as a critical component in gaining necessary skills and experience as a composer. Even if they use software to notate compositions, students benefit most from hearing compositions played by their peers, who can accurately evaluate composition strengths and areas for improvement.

Motivation

Student motivation provides another reason for student composers and their peers to perform their compositions. These compositions have social significance as well as real-world relevance, and students have greater concern for composition if other ensemble members perform and evaluate it. In accounting for social learning styles, I sometimes let students work together on assignments if I feel it motivates particular students.

I further motivate students (and get support from families) by encouraging students to perform their compositions for family members in preparation for the lesson in which they will perform their piece. I highly recommend that beginners perform for their parents weekly, and even have students indicate on their weekly practice records if they have done so. These performances have even more meaning if a student plays his or her own composition. For example, Giana proudly titled one of her compositions "Farming Circle" (a method of farming in which tasks are divided amongst a group) because of feedback her mother gave her.

The opportunity for expression also motivates some students. For example, in one lesson group Saquan titled his composition "Kirk Park" in reference to his football team, which served as the inspiration for the spirited and bombastic style of the piece. In the same lesson group, Malaysia titled her composition "Semaj" (see Figure 8.7 later in the chapter) in honor of her younger sister. The settings students choose for pieces serve as sources of compositional ideas as well as relevant expressions of students' lives.

SOME HELPFUL TIPS

To avoid transposition and time issues, I give short composition assignments for younger musicians to play and evaluate during homogeneous lesson groups. In programs where there is no small-group instruction, directors can transpose student compositions (computer software does this quickly) so the whole group can play, or small groups of students with homogeneous instruments can perform while others evaluate.

In order to ensure success, tasks begin with a high degree of structure and gradually require more student knowledge of notation and music theory, and compositional freedom increases with subsequent assignments. Because time is always critical, I expect carefully and legibly written compositions so that we may use them as études as well as composition activities during lessons or rehearsals.

Figure 8.4 shows a beginning activity where the student finishes the melody using C, D, E, F, and G pitches and quarter note and half note

Figure 8.4   Melody activity

Figure 8.5   Example of student work

durations. Students might complete the composition and prepare for its performance together. Figure 8.5 is an example of student work.

Of course, improvisation and composition assignments can be modified depending on the needs of the students. For example, a student percussionist with severe cognitive challenges may only improvise rhythms. The director should choose other students in the section to improvise melodies on keyboard percussion instruments while the exceptional learner echoes and improvises on drums. Figure 8.6 is a beginning composition activity (see Figure 8.4) modified for an exceptional learner who has difficulty reading notation. The duration of notes may be shown graphically by drawing dashes under the notes (as shown). You can also color code notes to help students identify them.

For advanced beginners, use a less structured composition assignment. Provide a blank staff and have students compose a short piece for their particular instrument, using the rhythms and pitches they have learned. I encourage students to keep it simple and to write neatly so that they and the other members of the group can easily read and perform the song. Figure 8.7 is an example of student work.

Directors should design composition assignments that focus on specific skills to reinforce performance and reading as students and peers play through pieces. For example, students may be given an assignment to compose a four-bar étude that uses slurs.

It often takes one or two weeks of revising before performing a composition in the lesson or rehearsal. Directors might need to reassign a com-

Figure 8.6   Beginning composition activity

Figure 8.7   Example of student work

position for individual students if it is illegible, has wide intervallic leaps, or has notation mistakes so that they don't waste precious time when "reading it down." Students will soon realize that revision is a necessary component of composing. If individual students require significant revisions, directors should try to conference with those students privately to avoid peer scrutiny. As long as sensitive directors create an encouraging environment and respect and value students' efforts, students do not feel humiliated when they must revise compositions.

To save time, compositions by every student need not be performed every week, though all should receive feedback. This feedback, whether by director or peers, should both acknowledge accomplishment as well as offer constructive critique. Evaluate compositions by using rubrics or other effective evaluation criteria clearly communicated to students when first giving the assignment.

Though I evaluate every composition assignment, to save time I note which student pieces have been played in the group to ensure that all students have pieces played by peers. The compositions that students play depend on the progress of individual students in the group. For example, Sonimar's piece titled "The Goal" (Figure 8.5) served as an exemplar for other students in her lesson group when they needed another week to revise their compositions. The following week, two revised compositions were performed. Sometimes I choose certain compositions because of their effectiveness in reinforcing other learning goals. Malaysia's composition was similar to a bass line in a piece that students were learning at the time, so they played "Semaj" (Figure 8.7) to reinforce it.

There is usually enough time for students to perform two short, legible, and otherwise error-free compositions during the typical lesson or rehearsal. I do not plan composition activities at certain times of the year, particularly around festival season and toward the beginning and end of the school year. Directors can plan composition assignments based on projected performance demands prior to the start of the school year and adjust plans as needed.

The following resources have helpful ideas on improvising and composing:

- Azzara, C. D., & Grunow, R. F. (2006). *Developing musicianship through improvisation*.
- Froseth, J. O., & Froseth, D. (1995). *Do it! Improvise I* and *Do it! Improvise II: In all the modes*.
- Hamann, D. L., & Gillespie, R. (2004). Practical approaches to teaching improvisation in the school orchestra. *In Strategies for teaching strings: Building a successful string and orchestra program*.
- Lieberman, J. L. (2002). *The creative band and orchestra*.

Improvisational and compositional activities reward your students when they realize their creative and expressive potential. Learning how to improvise and compose reinforces what players are learning, preparing them even better for performance.

Afterword

Some directors look for easy, quick fixes, but like most solutions to challenging issues in music education, many of the solutions I offer require diligence and patience. Directors may say they simply do not have the time to improve existing conditions in which they teach. These directors often mean that they are not willing to devote the time outside school hours to put new ideas into practice. Though directors who devote too much time to their jobs burn out, they need to diligently devote time outside class to plan, administrate, provide extra student instruction, foster parent and community relations, and tend to their own professional development, practice, and reflection. Directors also need patience because many improvements are gradual.

To meet challenges, I draw from sound teaching and learning principles that apply to all instrumental music settings. Nonetheless, I cannot help but recommend some context-specific practices from my own teaching experience that align with my personal teaching philosophy. Even if individual circumstances preclude adoption of some of my strategies, I hope that I demonstrate that either adapting established methods and techniques or creating new ones can provide solutions in any teaching environment. I encourage you to do the same.

I also hope that this book fosters or replenishes the tenacity in directors who work in less-than-ideal circumstances or deal with difficult challenges, as most directors do. I have certainly worked in unfavorable conditions and faced seemingly insurmountable challenges. I made those conditions better and solved tough problems through committed, sustained effort—because my students were worth it. Maintaining excellent, inclusive instrumental music programs in all school environments that serve all children regardless of privilege requires hard work.

Sharing the personal and musical rewards with students makes it all worthwhile.

Fight on! Your students need you.

References

Accent Music Instruments, LLC, Pilafian, S., Swoboda, D., LaDuke, L., & Wright, D. (Producers) (2005). *Band Blast off: Launch your band program* [DVD]. (Available from Focus on Excellence, 1955 W. Baseline Rd., Ste. 113-181, Mesa, AZ 85202; Phone: 480.233.2514, 800.332.2637; http://focus-on-music.com).

Adamek, M. S., & Darrow, A. (2005). *Music in special education*. Silver Spring, MD: The American Music Therapy Association, Inc.

Armstrong, T. A. (1999). *ADD/ADHD alternatives in the classroom*. Alexandria, VA: Association for Supervision and Curriculum Development.

Azzara, C. D. (1993). Audiation-based improvisation techniques and elementary instrumental students' music achievement. *Journal of Research in Music Education, 41*(4), 328–42.

Azzara, C. D., & Grunow, R. F. (2006). *Developing musicianship through improvisation*. Chicago: GIA Publications.

Azzara, C. D., Grunow, R. F., & Gordon, E. E. (1997). *Creativity in improvisation: Book 1*. Chicago: GIA Publications.

Bailey, B. B. (2001). *Conscious discipline: 7 basic skills for brain smart classroom management*. Oviedo, FL: Loving Guidance, Inc.

Baines, L. (2008). *A teacher's guide to multisensory learning: Improving literacy by engaging the senses*. Alexandria, VA: Association for Supervision and Curriculum Development.

Battisti, F., & Garofalo, R. (1990). *Guide to score study for the wind band conductor*. Ft. Lauderdale, FL: Meredith Music Publications.

Blocher, L. R., & Miles, R. B. (1999). *Scheduling and teaching music*. Springfield, IL: Focus on Excellence.

Bluestine, E. (2000). *The ways children learn music: An introduction and practical guide to Music Learning Theory*. Chicago: GIA Publications, Inc.

Boardman, E. (Ed.). (2002). *Dimensions of musical learning and teaching: A different kind of classroom*. Reston, VA: MENC.

Boyle, J. D., DeCarbo, N. J., & Jordan, D. M. (1995). Middle or junior high school band directors' views regarding reasons for student dropouts in instrumental music. Retrieved May 22, 2006, from http://music.arts.usf.edu/rpme/boyledec.htm.

Boyle, J. D., & Radocy, R. E. (1987). *Measurement and evaluation of musical experiences*. New York: Schirmer Books.

Brooks, J. G., & Brooks, M. G. (1993). *In search of understanding: The case for constructivist classrooms*. Alexandria, VA: Association for Supervision and Curriculum Development.

Brophy, T. S. (2000). *Assessing the developing child musician: A guide for general music teachers*. Chicago: GIA Publications.

Campbell, P. S., & Scott-Kassner, C. (1995). *Music in childhood: From preschool through the elementary grades*. New York: Schirmer.

Canter, L. (2006). *Lee Canter's classroom management for academic success*. Bloomington, IN: Solution Tree.

Casey, J. L. (1993). *Teaching techniques and insights for instrumental music educators* (Rev. ed.). Chicago: GIA Publications.

Celli-Sarasin, L. (1999). *Learning style perspectives: Impact in the classroom*. Madison, WI: Atwood Publishing.

Clark, C. A., & Chadwick, D. M. (1980). *Clinically adapted instruments for the multiply handicapped*. Saint Louis, MO: MMB Music.

Coffield, F., Moseley, D., Hall, E., & Ecclestone, K. (2004). *Learning styles and pedagogy in post-16 learning: A systematic and critical review*. Retrieved January 3, 2011, from http://hull.ac.uk/php/edskas/learning%20styles.pdf.

Colarusso, R., & O'Rourke, C. (2004). *Special education for all teachers* (3rd ed.). Dubuque, IA: Kendall/Hunt Publishing.

Comer, J. P. (2004). *Leave no child behind: Preparing today's youth for tomorrow's world*. New Haven, CT: Yale University Press.

Conn-Selmer. (n.d.). *Selmer Music Guidance Survey*. Available from Conn-Selmer, Inc., A Steinway Musical Instruments Company, P. O. Box 310, Elkhart, IN 46515. Telephone: 800-348-7426 or 574-522-1675. Website: www.selmer.com/content/educators.php.

Cutietta, R. A. (Ed.). (1999). *Strategies for teaching specialized ensembles*. Reston, VA: MENC.

Dalby, M. F. (1993). *Band rehearsal techniques: A handbook for new directors*. Northfield, IL: Instrumentalist Publishing Company.

Dunn, R., Debello, T., Brennan, P., Krimsky, J., & Murrain, P. (1981, December). Learning style researchers differences differently. *Educational Leadership*, 372–75. Retrieved on January 5, 2011, from www.ascd.org/ASCD/pdf/journals/ed_lead/el_198102_dunn.pdfdefine.

Elliott, D. J. (1995). *Music matters: A new philosophy of music education*. New York: Oxford University Press.

Fay, J. & Funk, D. (1995). *Teaching with love and logic*. Golden, CO: Love and Logic Press, Inc.

Feldstein, S. (1994). First performance: A demonstration concert: Beginning orchestra. Distributed by the Music Achievement Council, 5790 Armada Drive, Carlsbad, CA 92008. Telephone: 800-767-6266 or 760-438-8001. Website: www.musicachievementcouncil.org.

———. (2000). First performance: A demonstration concert: Beginning instrumental music [band]. Distributed by the Music Achievement Council, 5790 Armada Drive, Carlsbad, CA 92008. Telephone: 800-767-6266 or 760-438-8001. Website: www.musicachievementcouncil.org.

Fleming, N. D. (1995). I'm different, not dumb. Modes of presentation (VARK) in the tertiary classroom. In A. Zelmer (Ed.), *Research and development in higher education: Proceedings of the 1995 annual conference of the Higher Education and Research Development Society of Australia (HERDSA)*, Vol. 18, pp. 308–13.

Froseth, J. O., & Froseth, D. (1995a). *Do it! Improvise I.* Chicago: GIA Publications.

———. (1995b). *Do it! Improvise II: In all the modes.* Chicago: GIA Publications.

Gardner, H. (1999). *Intelligence reframed: Multiple intelligences for the 21st century.* New York: Basic Books.

Gordon, E. E. (1984). *Instrument timbre preference test.* Chicago: GIA Publications.

———. (1997). *Learning sequences in music: Skill, content, and patterns: A music learning theory.* Chicago: GIA Publications.

Grinder, M. (1993). *Envoy: Your personal guide to classroom management.* Battle Ground, WA: Michael Grinder and Associates.

Grunow, R. F., & Gordon, E. E. (1989). *Jump right in: The instrumental series, teacher's guide, book one.* Chicago: GIA Publications.

Hale, J. E. (2001). *Learning while black: Creating educational excellence for African American children.* Baltimore: Johns Hopkins University Press.

Hamann, D. L., & Gillespie, R. (2004). *Strategies for teaching strings: Building a successful string and orchestra program.* Oxford, UK: Oxford University Press.

Hammel, A. M. & Hourigan, R. M. (2011). *Teaching music to students with special needs: A label-free approach.* New York, NY: Oxford University Press.

IDEA. Pub. L. No. 94-142 (1975).

Jones, F. (2000). *Tools for teaching: Discipline, instruction, motivation.* Santa Cruz, CA: Frederic H. Jones & Associates, Inc.

Kaplan, P. R., & Stauffer, S. L. (1994). *Cooperative learning in music.* Reston, VA: MENC.

Kohn, A. (1999). *Punished by rewards: The trouble with gold stars, incentive plans, A's, praise, and other bribes.* New York: Houghton Mifflin Company.

Kohut, D. L. (1996). *Instrument music pedagogy: Teaching techniques for school band and orchestra directors.* Champaign, IL: Stipes Publishing.

Kunjufu, J. (1986). *Motivating and preparing Black youth to work.* Chicago: African American Images.

———. (1990). *Countering the conspiracy to destroy Black boys,* Vol. III. Chicago: African American Images.

———. (2002). *Black students. Middle class teachers.* Chicago: African American Images.

———. (2005). *Keeping black boys out of special education.* Chicago: African American Images.

Kuykendall, C. (1992). *From rage to hope: Strategies for reclaiming Black and Hispanic students.* Bloomington, IN: National Education Service.

Ladson-Billings, G. (1994). *The dreamkeepers: Successful teachers of African American children.* San Francisco: Jossey-Bass Publishers.

Lamb, N. (1990). *Guide to teaching strings* (5th ed.). Dubuque, IA: Wm. C. Brown.

Landis, B., & Carder, P. (1990). The Dalcroze approach. In P. Carder (Ed.), *The eclectic curriculum in American music education* (pp. 7–29). Reston, VA: MENC.

Lieberman, J. L. (2002). *The creative band and orchestra*. New York: Huiksi Music.

Lisk, E. S. (2001). *The creative director: Beginning and intermediate levels*. Galesville, MD: Meredith Music Publications.

Madsen, C. H., Jr., & Madsen, C. K. (1983). *Teaching/discipline*. Raleigh, NC: Contemporary Publishing Company.

McPherson, G. E., and Gabrielsson, A. (2002). From sound to sign. In R. Parncutt & G. E. McPherson (Eds.), *The science and psychology of music performance: Creative strategies for teaching and learning* (pp. 99–115). Oxford, UK: Oxford University Press.

MENC. (1989). *Music booster manual*. Reston, VA: MENC.

———. (1994). *The school music program: A new vision*. Reston, VA: MENC.

Mendler, A. N. (2001). *Connecting with students*. Alexandria, VA: Association for Supervision and Curriculum Development.

Mendler, B. D., Curwin, R. L., & Mendler, A. N. (2008). *Strategies for successful classroom management: Helping students succeed without losing your dignity or sanity*. Thousand Oaks, CA: Corwin Press.

Middleton, J., Haines, H., & Garner, G. (1998). *The band director's companion*. San Antonio, TX: Southern Music Company.

Mixon, K. (2009). Engaging and educating students with culturally responsive performing ensembles. *Music Educators Journal, 95*(4), 66–73.

Moore, M. C., with Batey, A. L., & Royse, D. M. (2002). *Classroom management in general, choral, and instrumental music programs*. Reston, VA: MENC.

Moss Rehabilitation Hospital Settlement Music School Therapeutic Music Program. (1982). *Guide to the selection of musical instruments with respect to physical ability and disability*. Saint Louis, MO: MMB Music, Inc.

Music Achievement Council. (n.d.). *Musical instrument game*. Available from Music Achievement Council, 5790 Armada Drive, Carlsbad, CA 92008. Telephone: 800-767-6266 or 760-438-8001. Website: www.musicachievementcouncil.org.

Ogbu, J. U. (1992). Understanding cultural diversity and learning. *Educational Researcher, 21*(8), 5–14.

O'Neill, S. A., & McPherson, G. E. (2002). Motivation. In R. Parncutt & G. E. McPherson (Eds.), *The science and psychology of music performance: Creative strategies for teaching and learning* (pp. 31–46). Oxford, UK: Oxford University Press.

Pashler, H., McDaniel, M., Rohrer, D., & Bjork, R. (2008). Learning styles: Concepts and evidence. *Psychological Science in the Public Interest, 9*(3), 103–19. Retrieved January 5, 2011, from http://bjorklab.psych.ucla.edu/pubs/Pashler_McDaniel_Rohrer_Bjork_2009_PSPI.pdf.

Payne, R. K. (2001). *A framework for understanding poverty* (new rev. ed.). Highlands, TX: aha! Process, Inc.

———. (2006). *Working with parents: Building relationships for student success*. Highlands, TX: aha! Process, Inc.

Reimer, B. (1989). *A philosophy of music education* (2nd ed.). Englewood Cliffs, NJ: Prentice-Hall.

Sax, L. (2005). *Why gender matters: What parents and teachers need to know about the emerging science of sex differences.* New York: Broadway Books.

Schleuter, S. L. (1997). *A sound approach to teaching instrumentalists* (2nd ed.). New York: Schirmer Books.

Shaw, V. (1992). *Community building in the classroom.* San Clemente, CA: Kagan.

Steinberg, L. (1996). *Adolescence* (4th ed.). New York: McGraw-Hill.

Taylor, J. A., Barry, N. H., & Walls, K. S. (1997). *Music and students at risk: Creative solutions for a national dilemma.* Reston, VA: MENC.

Udvari-Solner, A., & Kluth, P. (2008). *Joyful learning: Active and collaborative learning in inclusive classrooms.* Thousand Oaks, CA: Corwin Press.

Westphal, F. W. (1990). *Guide to teaching woodwinds* (5th ed.). Dubuque, IA: Wm. C. Brown Publishers.

Wilson, B. L., & Corbett, H. D. (2001). *Listening to urban kids: School reform and the teachers they want.* Albany: State University of New York Press.

Wong, H. K., & Wong, R. T. (2005). *The first days of school.* Mountain View, CA: Harry K. Wong Publications, Inc.

Zdzinski, S. F. (2003). Instrumental music for special learners. In MENC, *Readings on diversity, inclusion, and music for all* (pp. 120–23). Reston, VA: MENC.

About the Author

Kevin Mixon began his career in rural and suburban schools in Illinois and spent several years teaching in urban schools in New York State. His instrumental groups consistently received the highest ratings at regional festivals and were widely recognized for achievement. He is currently the fine arts director for the Syracuse City School District. Mixon earned degrees summa cum laude at Onondaga Community College, Syracuse University, University of Illinois–Urbana-Champaign, and the State University of New York at Oswego. Mr. Mixon presents sessions internationally at conventions including the International Society for Music Education World Conference, the Midwest Clinic, and MENC regional and national conferences. Several of his articles have appeared in *Music Educators Journal, Teaching Music, The Instrumentalist,* and *The National Band Association Journal,* and he is a contributing author to *Teaching Music in the Urban Classroom: A Guide to Survival, Success, and Reform* (MENC and Rowman & Littlefield Education). His highly acclaimed compositions for band and orchestra are available through Alfred Publishing, Kendor Music, and Carl Fischer Music.